A Great Basin Mosaic

Wilbur S. Shepperson Series in Nevada History
Series Editor: Michael Green (UNLV)

Nevada is known politically as a swing state and culturally as a swinging state. Politically, its electoral votes have gone to the winning presidential candidate in all but one election since 1912 (it missed in 1976). Its geographic location in the Sunbelt; an ethnically diverse, heavily urban, and fast-growing population; and an economy based on tourism and mining make it a laboratory for understanding the growth and development of postwar America and post-industrial society. Culturally, Nevada has been associated with legal gambling, easy divorce, and social permissiveness. Yet the state also exemplifies conflicts between image and reality: it also is a conservative state yet depends heavily on the federal government; its gaming regulatory system is the envy of the world but resulted from long and difficult experience with organized crime; its bright lights often obscure the role of organized religion in Nevada affairs. To some who have emphasized the impact of globalization and celebrated or deplored changing moral standards, Nevada reflects America and the world; to others, it affects them.

This series is named in honor of one of the state's most distinguished historians, author of numerous books on the state's immigrants and cultural development, a longtime educator, and an advocate for history and the humanities. The series welcomes manuscripts on any and all aspects of Nevada that offer insight into how the state has developed and how its development has been connected to the region, the nation, and the world.

A Great Basin Mosaic

The Cultures of Rural Nevada

JAMES W. HULSE

UNIVERSITY OF NEVADA PRESS *Reno & Las Vegas*

Wilbur S. Shepperson Series in Nevada History

University of Nevada Press, Reno, Nevada 89557 USA
www.unpress.nevada.edu
Cover design by Louise OFarrell

LIBRARY OF CONGRESS CATALOGING-IN-PUBLICATION DATA
Names: Hulse, James W., author.
Title: A Great Basin mosaic : the cultures of rural Nevada /
James W. Hulse.
Description: Reno : University of Nevada Press, 2016. | Includes
bibliographical references and index.
Identifiers: LCCN 2016038477 (print) | LCCN 2016051980 (ebook) |
ISBN 978-1-943859-25-2 (paperback : alkaline paper) |
ISBN 978-0-87417-466-3 (ebook)
Subjects: LCSH: Nevada—History, Local. | Great Basin—History,
Local. | Cities and towns—Nevada—History. | Counties—Nevada—
History. | Community life—Nevada—History. | Nevada—Social life
and customs. | Nevada—Rural conditions. | Local government—
Nevada—History. | Nevada—Economic conditions.
Classification: LCC F841 .H76 2016 (print) | LCC F841 (ebook) |
DDC979.3—dc23
LC record available at https://lccn.loc.gov/2016038477

This book has been reproduced as a digital reprint.

Manufactured in the United States of America

Contents

Acknowledgments   vii

Introduction   3

1. Two Passageways Across the Basin   14

2. Nevada Territory and Early Statehood, 1861–1869,
   Unionville and Austin   20

3. Railroad Stations along the Humboldt Trail   26
   Big Meadows, Winnemucca, Battle Mountain,
   Carlin, Elko, and Wells

4. Nineteenth-Century Towns of the Middle Corridor   35
   Belmont, Pahranagat, Hamilton, Pioche, Panaca,
   and Eureka

5. The Politics of Conscience   51
   Silver Crusade, Native American Policy,
   and Woman Suffrage

6. Turn of the Century   58
   Economics and Culture

7. Government Experiments in Churchill County   65

8. Copper Is King   87
   New Technology in White Pine County

9. A Lifeline for the Southeast   97
   Clark's Railroad

10. The MX Missile Controversy, 1978–81, and
    the Thirty-Five-Year Water War, 1980–2015   103

11. Lovelock, Winnemucca, and Battle
    Mountain Revisited   109

12. New Agendas for Elko County   115
    Tourists, Entertainment, Gold

13. Changing Landscapes in the Twentieth Century   125

14. Spanning the Distances, Part One   131
    Newspapers, Schools, and Churches

15. Spanning the Distances, Part Two   145
    Connecting the North-Center to the Nation

    Appendix: Changing Demographics, 1900–2010   151

    Bibliography   153

    About the Author   161

    Index   163

Illustrations follow page 74

Acknowledgments

The roster of people who have given help to this eclectic prospector is long. Most of them may not have known of their contributions or that their insights would be winnowed into an essay later on. In many cases, neither did I. One of my favorite hobbies has been to stop along the way in my rambles to read the local newspapers and promotional pieces and to listen to the locals—many of whom have been long-time friends. The people in the chambers of commerce, libraries, and government offices often yield information that extends beyond the moment.

But in my half-century of research and writing on Nevada, I have accumulated many intellectual debts to colleagues, friends, and especially librarians. A special acknowledgment must go to the staff of the University of Nevada–Reno library (now known as the Mathewson–IGT Knowledge Center). Their Special Collections department contains the best-organized and most accessible collection of Nevadiana. The staff members, both professional and part-time, are well prepared to help with questions of all kinds. Over the years, the personnel at the Nevada Historical Society, and at the Nevada State Library and Archives in Carson City, have repeatedly come to my rescue. The excellent public libraries at Reno, Elko, Ely, Winnemucca, Lovelock, and Fallon have unique resources that have served me well. Among the most informative museums for my purposes were the Northeastern Nevada Museum in Elko and the Churchill County Museum in Fallon.

This mosaic offers a supplement to two important recent volumes on Nevada. Cheryll Glotfelty of the University of Nevada–Reno has harvested much fruit from writers with her collection in *Literary Nevada* (2008). Michael S. Green of the University of Nevada–Las Vegas, in his 2015 opus *Nevada: A History of the Silver*

State, has broadened our perspectives, especially of Clark County. But as he acknowledges, his book does little to survey the evolving story of the rural north. I offer this work as a bridge between such mega-histories and the local remembrances offered by those who inhabit the thinly populated expanse of the North-Center.

Near the completion of this project, the work of William L. Fox, *Mapping the Empty: Eight Artists and Nevada*, came to mind. Those profiled in his pages are engaged in a more sensitive and creative process than my work can aspire to achieve, but their works also offer attempts to engage us in the mosaic that is Nevada.

This manuscript evolved over several years, as retirement leisure permitted more wanderings into the landscape of the mosaic. For a while, it languished at the University of Nevada Press and then was revived at the invitation of a new generation of editors and designers. My thanks this time goes to Justin Race, the new director, a worthy successor to Bob Laxalt.

Among the people who offered insights and crucial help in the last phases of the manuscript's gestation were Michon and Mike Mackedon and Kirk Robertson of Fallon; Wallie Cuchine of Eureka; my nephew Russell Jones of Winnemucca; my brother Frank Hulse of Pioche; Jack Hursh, Rose Strickland, and Dennis Ghiglieri of Reno; Sean Pitts of Ely; and Cyd McMullen and David Roche of Elko.

Finally, thanks go to my daughter Jane Dixon and daughter-in-law Cari Blomquist, who added some finishing touches, and to my most patient and dedicated critic, Betty, who has learned the twenty-first century techniques of editing and photography in their many facets.

A Great Basin Mosaic

Introduction

What does the word "Nevada" mean in the idiom of the twenty-first century? When non-Nevadans hear the term these days, the images that arise involve gambling and cheap or expensive entertainment—glittering casinos, world-class floorshows, or perhaps the Burning Man festival on the Black Rock Desert. For several decades, such superficial impressions have been tattooed on the skin of the so-called Silver State.

Yet there is a deeper landscape in the outlying, mostly rural expanse. In 1974, author Robert Laxalt offered this view in a perceptive article titled "The Other Nevada," published in the *National Geographic.* He referred to "the Nevada that has been eclipsed by the tinsel trimmings of Las Vegas, the round-the-clock hotel-casinos, the ski slopes of the Sierra. It is a Nevada that few tourists see.

"It is a Nevada of small communities," he continued, "livestock towns like Elko and Winnemucca, mining towns like Ely and Yerington, isolated ranches and a few Indian reservations, and ghost towns surrounded by an overpowering vastness of land" (Laxalt, 1974:7330).

In the pages that follow, I reflect on and modify Laxalt's insights. No single "other" Nevada exists, but several subcultures with distinct features can be found out there. Great changes have occurred in these "others" since he wrote his lyrical tribute more than forty years ago. Some are adapting to the technological revolutions of recent times. Others are surrendering to the primordial dust. But many places still have the characteristics he illuminated.

Twenty years after Laxalt's article, Ann Ronald and Stephen Trimble blended essays and photographs to produce *Earthtones: A Nevada Album* (1995). Ronald prospected in the remote mountains and valleys with her notepad and literary eye; Trimble carried his photographic equipment. Together, they achieved a sensitive, affectionate blend of images and tributes to the panorama

3

that Nature offers. Their work continues to give the twenty-first-century armchair explorer sensitive insights into what John Muir once called the "bewildering abundance" of the Nevada landscape.

My assumption in this book is that somewhere between the colorful natural backdrop of Ronald/Trimble and the noise of the growing cities another possibility exists. Let us consider the cultures of smaller towns and the professions that are dying and those that are emerging. The Nevadas of the lesser-known cities, towns, and outposts deserve their separate chronicles. The cultural variations of these other Nevadas have been short-changed by academic historians who consider the state as a whole. Fortunately, this neglect has been partly remedied by local writers, photographers, and researchers who work primarily on a county-by-county, town-by-town basis.

My contribution is informed by memories of tramping though rural Nevada as a child, then as a journalist in search of news and gossip, later as an academic historian and a parent trying to share the wonders of the high desert with family. I do not aspire to the aesthetic sensitivity of the artists previously mentioned. In the manner of members of my craft, I focus on the towns, including their mundane politics and economic situations, though occasionally I venture onto the quicksand of cultural and social analysis.

THE NORTH-CENTER

The area I have in mind embraces about 75,000 square miles, more than three-quarters of the state. It includes eight counties: Churchill, Elko, Humboldt, Lander, Eureka, White Pine, Pershing, and Lincoln. We will dip into the northern half of Nye County, but only briefly. Carson City, Reno and Las Vegas are on the distant periphery of this text. I label this region the "North-Center." "The other Nevada" might also serve, but others have used the term since Laxalt's time and it oversimplifies the cultural diversity.

The area in my range of vision is a large, thinly populated piece of western America. The two-thirds of Nevada considered here is a vast laboratory for the ongoing frontier experiment in a high-desert venue. It is still a frontier by the standard Frederick Jackson Turner set more than 120 years ago—it has fewer than two residents per square mile. Of course there are exceptions:

isolated urban islands such as Elko, Fallon, and Winnemucca that we will visit. But most of it is nearly as empty of people as it was a century ago.

The North-Center of my definition is bounded on the east by the Bonneville Salt Flats and on the west by the Black Rock Desert and its southern neighbor—the Forty-Mile Desert. For the northern border we take the 42nd parallel, which separates Nevada from Oregon and Idaho.

The southern boundary is more difficult to define. It is that wide swath where the high Great Basin topography blends into the Mojave Desert. This blurred transition zone allows us to include places like Belmont, Pioche, Panaca, Caliente, and Fallon but leaves the most famous boom camps of the early twentieth century— Tonopah and Goldfield— beyond our horizon. The rationale here is that these latter towns, in their prosperous and post-bonanza years, have received more attention from historians of the previous generation than the communities of the high basin. And they belong to the Mojave Desert, not the botanical high desert.

Stephen Trimble, in *The Sagebrush Ocean*, has provided a useful metaphor. He points out that there is not one single plant that fits into the category of "sagebrush" but a dozen varieties. The most widely distributed and best known is the *Artemisia tridentada*, distinguished by its purple leaves and its pungent aroma. It brings a nostalgic thrill to those of us who came of age within its zone but who have been deprived of its zest by long urban confinement.

We are dealing with a landscape that reveals a turbulent record of tectonic activity extending over a million years. Humans have lived here for only about 13,000 years. The so-called "western" peoples who originated in Europe have resided here for only about a century and a half, most of that time in miniscule numbers. Several generations of prospectors of various kinds have romped like grasshoppers through these parts, eager to consume and move on. Only a few have remained, until recently.

The six or seven generations of those who call themselves Nevadans have been on this turf during the time of recorded history. They have faced a fascinating challenge: adapt a version of western civilization to a setting that is not well designed for its ambitions. In these pages, we will examine the 150 years of that cultural experiment, mostly beyond the natural watershed of the Sierra Nevada.

In 1942, the social historian Richard Lillard, author of *Desert Challenge: An Interpretation of Nevada*, produced a free-flowing, affectionate description. He titled one of his chapters "California's Colony." This may have been an accurate label for the western and southwestern fringes of the state at the time, but it does not apply to the North-Center in the twenty-first century.

The story that unfolds in the following pages is mostly beyond the shadows of Reno, Carson City, and Las Vegas and far beyond the penumbra of California. Half of the North-Center basin is nearer to Salt Lake City and remote from all of the above. The history of the North-Center has long been a series of footnotes to the more exciting, more politically oriented narratives of events that occurred farther west in Carson City–Reno and south in the Las Vegas region. But these counties and towns have also been accumulating records of change that deserve separate attention. This book tries to build on, compare, and condense such local accounts. I approach the field as a late-coming scavenger in search of historical evidence, picking through the artifacts left by my predecessors and contemporaries.

THREE SEGMENTS

To begin, we look again at the region's history from 1860 to 1900, when the North-Center was little more than an unknown outback. This involves some reflection on the territorial and early state history. The focus here will be on the delicate economies of the North-Center and the most pressing social and cultural issues.

The second segment offers a county-by-county, town-by-town summary of local history, emphasizing the similarities and differences in cultural life among these widely scattered places with their often untraditional names. It seeks to define the local contexts with occasional backward glances at statewide agendas. North-Center became a domain where large livestock grazing enterprises could often make a profit—thanks to the proximity of the Central Pacific railroad—except when drought or freezing winters interfered. One point of focus will be the evolution of the huge cattle and sheep fiefdoms of the late nineteenth century. The federal laws initially intended to help homesteaders and small farmers instead gave bonuses to the livestock barons.

The third segment is more diverse and complex. It deals with the cultural evolution of these distinct places. It reflects on the efforts of local newspapers, schools, and religious groups to link their isolated communities to the larger society. One section deals with design and finance of roads, highways, and eventually freeways. Another considers the evolution of telephone communication and more recent electronic and media developments. Finally we consider the work of federal agencies to maintain and restore public lands.

Some of the later pages reflect on changing attitudes toward the state and federal governments. For many who settled these mountains and valleys in the nineteenth century, the capitol in Carson City was far away, a place that imposed few taxes and provided fewer services. The most important government was tangible in locally elected officers who did their occasional official business in the courthouse—a judge, district attorney, assessor, sheriff, clerk, and treasurer. These officers were initially housed in a makeshift building, but as the years passed and as the anointed county seats became more stable, the courthouses became the tangible symbols of local authority and pride.

Washington and the federal government, if considered at all in the nineteenth century, were on a distant planet, most notably present on the Fourth of July when flags and whiskey enhanced the celebrations. The few laws that Congress had enacted about the public lands were only vaguely known. Aside from the government's grants to the railroad and several forts built to watch the Indians, federal authority existed only in the abstract—on paper. Nevadans elected to Congress were seldom seen or heard from again in the remote settlements of the North-Center until the next election. The absence of government became an article of faith. Even the state government in Carson City was mostly beyond the horizon of local concerns, until recently.

Whatever we individuals may think of the federal government in the twenty-first century—whether it's helpful or intrusive, friend or enemy—we might reflect on what it has done in the North-Center. We may not recall how the New Deal of the 1930s boosted these impoverished counties toward economic diversity. When the banks, miners, and cowmen were all in trouble, manna from the federal government lifted Nevada up. "The Feds" played a more constructive role in twentieth-century rural Nevada than is recognized in the toxic atmosphere of the twenty-first. As the presence of "the Feds" has expanded, their work has become more controversial. We will discuss Newlands project, the New Deal efforts to protect and develop resources, then proceed to the "Sagebrush Rebellion" and other, more recent controversies.

It's a mixed scenario. The "other Nevadas" include many ghost towns and a few former boomtowns that are struggling to avoid the same fate. We will linger in a few prosperous medium-sized cities—such as Elko, Winnemucca, and Fallon—that seem to be achieving economic diversification that the state has long sought, even as the larger cities cope with the aftermath of the Great Recession. We will also visit some places of marginal success and a few whose economic health is unstable.

In the 1930s, when I lived with my grandmother in Pioche, she occasionally set up a quilting frame in her bedroom, the biggest space in her clapboard house. Other grandmothers would come by with their rag pieces, and together they sewed a bedcover that might become a gift to a bride, a child, or someone in need. A visitor to the scattered museums of the western Great Basin—in Elko, Winnemucca, Lovelock, Fallon, Eureka, Ely, Tonopah, Pioche, and Caliente—might find visual and written examples of handicraft work of this kind.

If one lingers for a while among the memorabilia of the North-Center, she or he will find scraps of fabric from which a prose quilt might be fashioned. Much of the cutting and stitching has been done by local historians. Here, I will try to adapt my grandmother's art of bringing seemingly disparate pieces together into a larger pattern in a different medium.

Finally, I do not aspire to describe the Native American subcultures of the Native Americans that have inhabited this landscape. There are two reasons for this. First, I am incapable of doing justice to these peoples; and second, their stories and achievements have been so richly described by others and are so well illustrated in our newer museums.

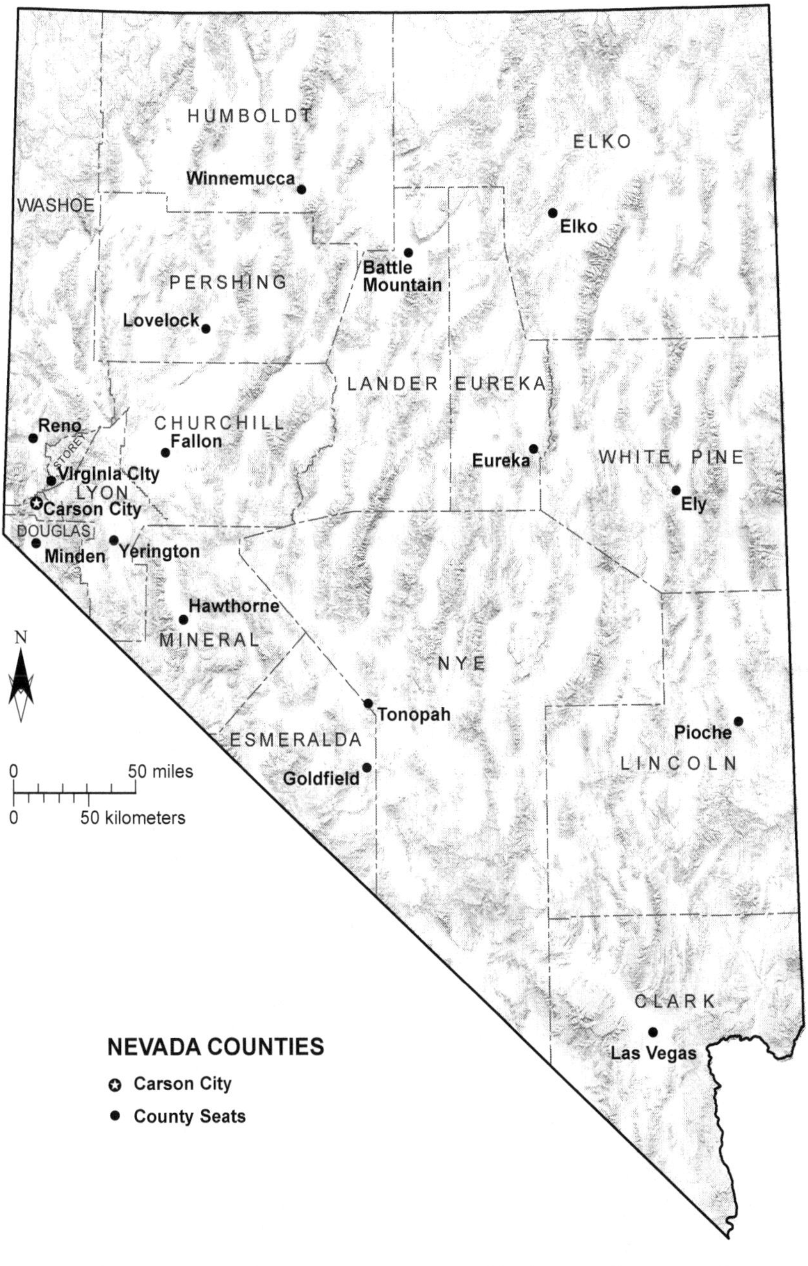
HUMBOLDT
ELKO
Winnemucca
WASHOE
Elko
Battle Mountain
PERSHING
Lovelock
LANDER
EUREKA
CHURCHILL
Reno
STOREY
Fallon
Eureka
WHITE PINE
Virginia City
LYON
Ely
Carson City
DOUGLAS
Minden
Yerington
Hawthorne
N
MINERAL
NYE
Tonopah
Pioche
ESMERALDA
LINCOLN
0
50 miles
Goldfield
0
50 kilometers
CLARK
Las Vegas
NEVADA COUNTIES
Carson City
County Seats

Nevada with county lines, county seats, and highways. Courtesy of Irene M. Seelye.

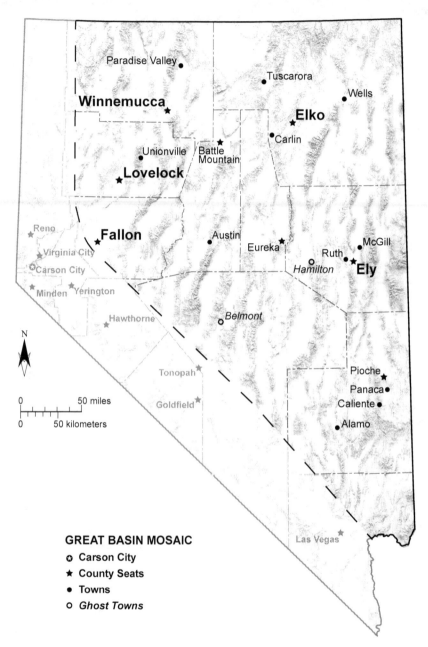

GREAT BASIN MOSAIC

- ✪ Carson City
- ★ County Seats
- ● Towns
- ○ *Ghost Towns*

Great Basin mosaic area with communities. Courtesy of Irene M. Seelye.

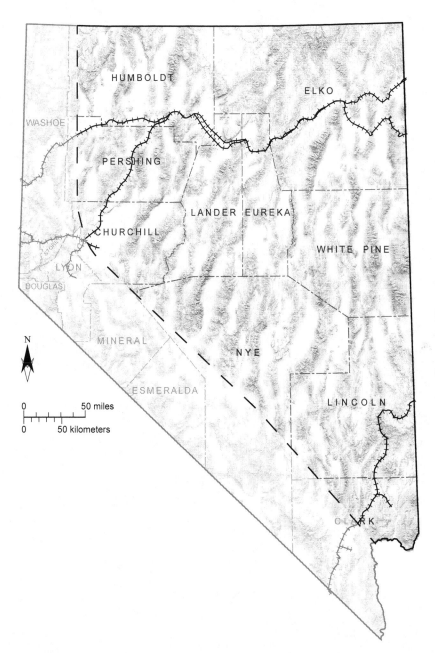

Great Basin mosaic railroads. Courtesy of Irene M. Seelye.

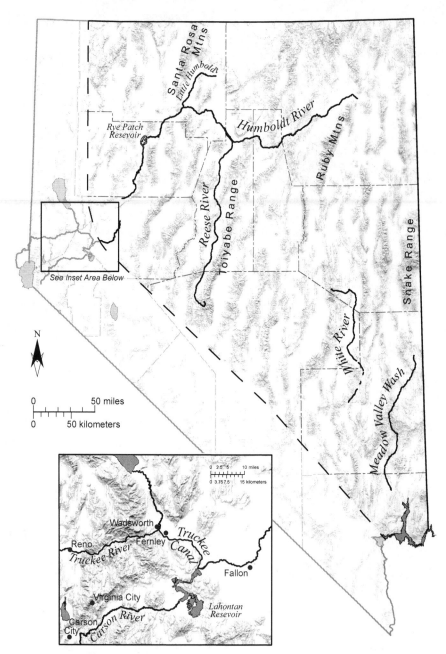

Great Basin mosaic rivers and major mountain ranges. Courtesy of
Irene M. Seelye.

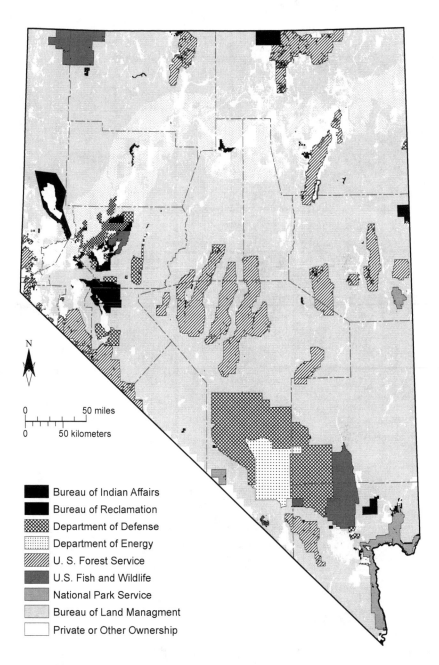

Nevada land use. Courtesy of Irene M. Seelye.

CHAPTER ONE

Two Passageways Across the Basin

The Great Basin offered two main routes for the explorers and emigrants who crossed the terrain between the Rocky Mountains and central California in the 1840s and 50s. Most emigrants chose the Humboldt Trail. It was well mapped but hazardous because of the fickle water supply. The alternative—the Center—was a more rugged tangle of options across the midriff of the Basin. It was explored several times for faster passage—for example by the Pony Express.

These choices were still available to motorists in 2016. The Humboldt route was the overwhelming favorite because it is relatively level. It was chosen for the first transcontinental railroad in the 1860s (the Central Pacific west of Utah) and as the main east-west corridor—the Eisenhower Highway (I-80)—in the 1950s.

Approximately a hundred miles south of the Humboldt trail is U.S. Route 50, which was promoted in the 1920s as the Lincoln Highway. It has always been less popular but is more scenic because of its mountainous terrain.

THE HUMBOLDT RIVER ROUTE

The Humboldt River is the aorta of the northwestern Great Basin. This is a clumsy metaphor, because the Humboldt does not circulate. It meanders west through a parched desert for 300 miles before ending in an alkaline sink. It is a puny waterway, hardly worthy of being called a river, but it is the lifeblood of the northwestern Great Basin. Anglo–Americans first learned of it in the reports of the Canadian explorer Peter Skene Ogden, probing for the Hudson's Bay Company in the 1820s. He was looking for beaver, whose pelts brought high prices in European luxury markets. Ogden's traps did not snare many beaver in the Humboldt basin, but he lifted the curtain on an unknown segment of the North American continent for later explorers.

Scholars are uncertain how far Ogden penetrated into the southern desert, but recently recovered records indicate that he explored the Humboldt Basin three times between 1826 and 1830. The earliest maps based on his reports identify this stream as "Unknown River" or "Ogden's River."

Next, Joseph R. Walker led his semisecret, fact-finding mission to California on behalf of the U.S. Army in 1833 along the Humboldt when this region was part of Mexico. Official reports were ambiguous about his authority and intentions. Accompanied by about sixty men when he crossed the region west of the Great Salt Lake, he encountered a number of Native Americans.

At times, the Indians reportedly pilfered the expedition's beaver traps and other gear, and some of Walker's men wantonly killed several Natives as revenge. While Walker may have disapproved of such activities and punished the men when he learned of their conduct, this did not prevent a greater crisis in the lower Humboldt basin.

When the expedition arrived at the ponds of the Sink, Walker thought that large numbers of the Natives—in this case Northern Paiutes—were gathering at a distance and encircling their encampment. Perhaps the Native Americans had no experience of guns and their deadly possibilities. When Walker demonstrated how his guns could kill ducks at a far distance with great noise, the Paiutes briefly retreated. When they returned, Walker's men mowed them down by the dozens.

This slaughter became known to Anglo–Americans only in later years. The journals of some of Walker's men mentioned it, and the novelist Washington Irving described it as a wild western adventure. But the bloody episode lingered in the folklore of Native Americans for decades.

In spite of its challenges, the Humboldt corridor was the least arduous route across the most barren sections of the American west—between the Utah salt flats and the foothills of the Sierra Nevada. No better east-west corridor with a stream of fresh water is available anywhere near this parallel—ca. 40–41 degrees latitude— for several hundred miles north or south.

In the 1840s, another explorer with a crew of careful record-keepers and more sophisticated instruments defined the physical features of the region in greater detail. John Fremont, the American "pathfinder," made three extended probes into and across the region. He named it the "Great Basin," a land of interior drainage where the streams do not find an outlet to the sea. He also replaced "Ogden's River" on the maps with that of Alexander von Humboldt, the famous early nineteenth-century German explorer who never visited Nevada but whose reputation Fremont admired.

A few years after Fremont had defined the Basin, the Humboldt Trail became the preferred route for emigrant caravans on their way to California. It was on this route in the Sierras that the Donner Party of 1846 experienced its notorious disaster, which temporarily dampened eastern enthusiasm for a western paradise. But just three years later, reports of gold diggings in California aroused thousands. They came with their loaded wagons, unprepared for the journey across the prairies, the Rocky Mountains, the deserts of the Great Basin, and finally the Sierra Nevada.

Of them all, the Great Basin was the most dreaded challenge on the journey across the continent. The Humboldt River was a refreshing gift from the mountains for emigrants and their animals, especially when they arrived upstream in springtime. But the water meandered and became bitterly alkaline and polluted as later-arriving emigrants moved downstream toward the end of summer. They usually needed three or four weeks to make the trek down the Humboldt from its headwaters to the Sink. "This is the paradox of the Humboldt," Dale Morgan wrote in the early 1940s, "that it was almost the most necessary river of America, and the most hated."

After the emigrants had crossed the Sink, they faced the Forty-Mile Desert before arriving at the refreshing waters of the Truckee or Carson rivers. Then they faced the steep canyons and daunting summits of the Sierra Nevada.

Most emigrants of the 1850s, depending on carts and wagons pulled by oxen, chose the Carson route. For all the troubles and challenges the California Trail presented east and west of here, the Humboldt Basin was the most direct passageway for wheeled vehicles, as subsequent builders of railroads and interstate highways relearned many decades later.

As it flows for 250 miles, from the upstream tributaries above the town of Wells to the Sink south of Lovelock, the Humboldt drops only about 1,700 feet in elevation. Whatever other challenges the route presented to the traveler, extreme and abrupt slopes were the least important. This was not the case with the alternate routes farther south across the central expanse of the Great Basin.

THE WIDE AND RUGGED MIDDLE CORRIDOR

At about the same time Peter Ogden was making his first visit to the Humboldt River on behalf of his Canadian sponsors, a group of American rivals probed the more southern region.

Jedediah Smith and fourteen companions of the Rocky Mountain Fur Company approached the center of the Basin from the western side. In 1826, they had moved southward from the Great Salt Lake along the Wasatch Mountains to the Colorado River, which they followed into southern California. When Mexican authorities made it clear they were not welcome, Smith and two others started eastward in 1827 across the center of the Basin.

During that passage, they encountered successive mountain ranges—rugged uplands later named Shoshone, Toiyabe, Toquima, Monitor, Egan, Schell Creek, and Snake—and sighted many more. The southern part of the central Basin is an erratic sequence of towering, forested highlands with broad, apparently barren valleys in between.

Smith and his companions crossed the parched desert for about 300 miles toward the Snake Range by a route that many scholars have tried to reconstruct. The most dedicated historical sleuths believe the party must have gone through the Sacramento Pass (now the route of U.S. Highways 6 and 50) between Wheeler Peak and Mount Moriah). They barely survived the ordeal, apparently saved from death by helpful Native Americans, and eventually rejoined some of their companions near Bear Lake in the Wasatch Mountains.

When subsequent explorers probed westward south of the Great Salt Lake, several choices lay ahead. One of the most skillful scouts was Howard Egan, a Mormon who had been among the first settlers to arrive with Brigham Young in the Salt Lake valley in 1847. Egan, sometimes accompanied by two sons, was the first to document the various possibilities for crossing the Basin, with strong horses and sturdy men.

During the 1850s, several more small groups probed the central Basin in greater detail. By 1858, when Captain James H. Simpson received a commission from the U.S. Army to find a direct road from Camp Floyd, Utah, to central California, the approach had become more systematic. He assembled a team that included an artist-photographer, biologists, topographers and a geologist. The data recorded in his report were excellent, but it was completed just as the Civil War disrupted the national agenda. His records were not published until 1876.

By that time, many other observations were available in print, but Simpson left his name on one of the uplands, the Simpson Park Mountains. He identified the most prominent south-north tributary of the Humboldt River as the "Reese River," in honor of a guide who scouted for his crew. And notably, the Egan and Simpson information helped the most famous mail carriers of nineteenth-century America.

The Pony Express

In 1860, a new company promised to transport letters from St. Joseph, Missouri, to Sacramento in fewer than ten days. The Pony Express began offering its rapid mail service when geographical knowledge about the Basin was much improved but still sketchy. The riders and their ponies usually entered the Middle Corridor at Antelope Valley near the site of the present Goshute Indian Reservation.

The riders raced their steeds through a dozen mountain ranges and intervening valleys on their way to Carson City. The relay stations, where horses and riders could be changed, were usually 10 to 25 miles apart. This exciting experiment at rapid communication continued for only about eighteen months, but it left a rich legacy and a few crumbling rock buildings across the Corridor.

The Pony Express quickly became obsolete when the telegraph spanned the Basin in 1861–62. When the Clemens brothers, Orion and Samuel, rushed west in an Overland stagecoach during the summer of 1861, they arrived at a station on the Reese River and found a telegraph connection to Carson City, 180 miles farther west. The wire had been extended as far east as the Toiyabe mountains. Orion, the appointed Secretary of Nevada Territory, was able to tell Territorial Governor James W. Nye in Carson that he was on his way. The electronic revolution had made its first appearance in the central Basin.

The Overland Stage used approximately the same route as the Pony Express for several years during the 1860s, but it too became redundant and was finally abandoned when the Central Pacific railroad was completed in 1869.

THE TWO PASSAGES

Much later, in the twentieth century, the two routes established in the 1860s continued as the main passageways across the Great Basin. The Humboldt River corridor became U.S. Highway 40 and eventually, in the 1950s, Interstate 80 (the Eisenhower Highway). Its small variations in grade invited the heavy traffic of the age of gasoline- and diesel-powered vehicles.

Part of the central route defined by Egan, Simpson, and the Pony Express became Highway 50, currently promoted as the Lincoln Highway, or the Loneliest Road in America. Several of its passes are 7,000 feet high and offer the motorist many scenic variations of the Great Basin panorama at a slower pace than the accelerated traffic of I-80.

CHAPTER TWO

Nevada Territory and Early Statehood, 1861–1869, Unionville and Austin

When the members of the first Nevada territorial legislature met in Carson City late in 1861, they divided their new jurisdiction into nine counties. Defining such units in the western corner near Carson City and Virginia City was an easy task. Five promising little towns became county seats, looking forward to building courthouses and enjoying the other privileges that came with the launching of local governments.

The remaining part of the Territory sprawled over tens of thousands of square miles of the "Great East." Nobody knew much about the vast expanse between the Pyramid Lake and the eastern and southern boundaries. In their ignorance, legislators hastily drew lines on a map and divided this zone into three layers—Esmeralda, Churchill, and Humboldt counties.

The three units covered more than two-thirds of the Territory. Esmeralda County does not concern us here because most of it is in the Mojave Desert rather than in the sagebrush zone.

Churchill County was supposed to have its seat at Buckland's Station (a Pony Express and Overland Mail resting place) on the Carson River. This county had very few people, and its history before 1902 has little relevance to our narrative, except that within a year the eastern half was lopped off to create Lander County, with its theoretical seat at a place called Jacob's Station or Jacobsville on the Reese River.

The third eastern county—Humboldt—stretched across the entire northeastern corner of the Territory and had its original seat at Unionville, an ephemeral mining camp that we will soon visit in the company of Samuel L. Clemens.

As mentioned, the first legislators of Nevada Territory knew almost nothing about the resources and possibilities of the "Great East." However, Nevada's representatives in Washington soon

20

persuaded Congress to add two more vertical stretches of land, shifting the boundary more than 100 miles east, reducing Utah Territory, and south to the Colorado River at the expense of Arizona Territory. It was a landgrab enabled by ill-informed representatives working on totally ignorant members of Congress. County boundaries of the twenty-first century still reflect the hasty decisions of the 1860s.

UNIONVILLE

The earliest mining rush to the Humboldt region began in 1861 on the eastern slopes of the mountain range that borders the river. From the vantage of the territorial capitol in Carson City and the towns of the Comstock Lode, it was more than 100 miles away, back across the worst part of the Forty-Mile Desert. But rumors of rich ores were a magnet for restless young men who had failed to strike it rich in Virginia City.

Among the first excited greenhorns was Samuel L. Clemens, who had arrived from Missouri only a few weeks earlier with his brother, Orion, the appointed Secretary of Nevada Territory. After sizing up Carson City (then a tiny village) and the nearby regions of Lake Tahoe, Sam fell victim to the "gold and silver fever" that afflicted nearly all young men in the region.

As Clemens (who in the meantime had renamed himself Mark Twain) told the story later in *Roughing It*, he and three companions hiked across 150 miles of desert from Carson City to a place called Buena Vista Canyon where they expected to find nuggets of gold: "We had not less than thirty thousand 'feet' apiece in the 'richest mines on earth' as the frenzied cant phrased it—and we were in debt to the butcher. We were stark mad with excitement—drunk with happiness—smothered under mountains of prospective wealth—arrogantly compassionate toward the plodding millions who knew not our marvelous canyon—but our credit was not good at the grocer's."

The cold winter and their ignorance of metallurgy soon defeated Sam and his partners, so they rushed back toward Carson City to search for other possible bonanzas in the Sierra Nevada. And the Buena Vista district was a disappointment to three or four generations of miners and speculators who followed Clemens.

Unionville continued to be the seat of government for Humboldt County until 1873, although the county government lacked the money to construct a proper courthouse. Elected offices shifted from place to place and in some years issued scrip to pay the bills. A weekly newspaper was published locally from 1863 until 1869. Surviving files have allowed historians to conduct postmortem inquiries to supplement Twain's observations, but no mining production records survive from the territorial period. Production in later years was spotty at best. Mines recorded production only $2.6 million worth of ore during the next eighty years.

Unionville continues to be a tiny hamlet a century and a half after the mining excitement of the 1860s. The name "Buena Vista" reflected its setting in a canyon with a view eastward where the morning sun gilds the sagebrush with its first light and offers a serene backdrop to the valley. Those who remained in this place and their more Acadian successors planted orchards and gardens that flourished in the benign microclimate of the canyon. In the mid-twentieth century, it became a rustic retreat for urbanites seeking a quiet, remote second home.

AUSTIN

As Unionville's mining prospects dimmed, a sibling farther inland beckoned. The town of Austin in the Toiyabe Mountains was established soon after Unionville, but its lifespan has been much fuller. Pony Express riders based at the Jacobsville station on the Reese River picked at the rocks in the nearby foothills during their off-duty hours. When they discovered silver-bearing outcroppings in a narrow ravine called Pony Canyon, eight miles east of their station, word spread as quickly as seeds in the wind. Miners rushed in, and three or four tiny towns sprang up in 1862.

The legislature in Carson City, in session at the time, quickly authorized a new county named Lander in honor of Frederick W. Lander, a wagon-road builder. It originally included the entire northeastern corner of the Territory.

Austin became the focal point for frenzied prospectors who fanned out into the "Great East." The town experienced less gun-slinging anarchy than some camps of the same era, and it never suffered a fateful bust, because it did not have a real boom. It thus

auctioned several times, raising a substantial amount of money
for the charity.

The columns of the *Reveille* described these events in riveting
detail in the spring of 1864, and the excitement spread to Virginia
City, to San Francisco, and even (in a smaller afterglow) to East
Coast cities. Gridley's sack of flour became an icon for the town,
giving it more fame than its modest mineral wealth ever achieved.
Oscar Lewis, a popular and prolific writer of the mid-twentieth
century summarized Austin's place in history. He caught its enduring spirit with a book titled *The Town That Died Laughing*, first published in 1955. Austin was recognized as a generous, fun-loving
place more famous for its antics than its riches. This town—the
oldest and earliest in central Nevada—has also had the last laugh,
so far, because it has not yet died like a hundred of its offspring.
Some of its most impressive monuments are intact at this writing.

Austin's early Christian settlers had a taste for ecclesiastical
elegance. Three substantial churches, built in Pony Canyon in the
mid-nineteenth century were still standing in 2016, thanks in part
to support from parishioners elsewhere. Although the congregations that constructed and sustained them more than a century
ago have long since passed from the scene, the structures cling
to sides of the canyon in testimony to the faith and industry of
earlier generations.

Among the remnants of past ambitions is Stokes Castle, a
stone quadrangle that looms above the western approach to Pony
Canyon like the fragment of a medieval fortress. A three-story
tower, it was conceived and partly built more than a century ago by
wealthy members of the Anson Phelps Stokes family of Philadelphia, who had invested heavily in the local mines. They admired
the panoramic view westward across the Reese River Valley and
tried to replicate fortresses they had seen in Europe.

A contemporary settler who made his home there, Jim Anderson, wrote, "Austin, which seems at first glance like a changeless
little place modeled after a snow-village paperweight, is anything
but. That is where the surprise lies." Anderson and about 200 of
his fellow townsmen affirm that the magnificent view across the

avoided much of the extravagance that afflicted other mining centers in the 1870s. As the jumping-off point for several prospects
farther south and east, Lander came to be called the "mother of
counties." Austin might by the same logic be dubbed the parent
of new mining districts, since at least fifty more spawned farther
inland in the next two or three years according to the records of
the Nevada State Mineralogist for 1864–65.

Mineral production records show that mining districts near
Austin did not become important precious-metal producers during
the next hundred years. Official state accounts attribute only $18.5
million to the mines of the Reese River district between 1865 and
1940—a pittance when compared to several other districts that
came to life during the same era.

The first edition of its newspaper, the *Reese River Reveille*,
appeared in the spring of 1863 and survived for a century, despite
the town's faltering economy. The *Reveille* adopted an approach to
the news similar to that of the *Territorial Enterprise* of Virginia City,
where such notorious journalists as Mark Twain and Dan DeQuille
entertained their readers with frolic more often than fact.

One of the *Reveille's* early triumphs was a series of reports
about "Gridley's Sack of Flour" in the spring of 1864. Reuel C. Gridley was a grocer who had arrived early and established his business in "Upper Austin." He was a betting man who favored the
Confederate side in the Civil War. Although the war was a bloody
tragedy in the East and South, partisans in Nevada Territory could
make a friendly wager on a local election where a Yankee and a
Copperhead were opponents in a mayoral race. Gridley made a
bet with one of his pro-Union rivals on the outcome. The loser of
the bet was required to carry a 50-pound sack of flour the length
of Austin's Main Street, a steep grade more than a mile long. Gridley lost and was obliged to carry his burden, decorated with red-
white-and-blue bunting, before an assembled audience. Bands and
flags accompanied his performance.

Someone then proposed that the sack of flour should be auctioned again, with proceeds donated to the Sanitary Fund. This
agency (the predecessor of the American Red Cross) provided
care and treatment to wounded soldiers of both armies during
the Civil War. Popular interest in the contest grew, bringing more

Reese River Valley compensates for the isolation the town has known for 150 years.

So, unlike many of its central and eastern Nevada siblings, Austin has not joined the graveyard of ghost towns. It continues to attract residents who seek the rustic joys of an isolated village and who bring to it a stoic sense of humor. Although its residents are few, they have managed to maintain much of the light-hearted community spirit that Oscar Lewis described.

The main action in the North-Center was not on the old Pony Express Trail but farther north on the Humboldt Trail, where the powerful pioneers of American capitalism and transportation laid the rails of the Central Pacific Railroad. The cultural experiences that unfolded in the mining camps of the central corridor were quite different from those in the railroad towns farther north.

CHAPTER THREE

Railroad Stations along the Humboldt Trail

Big Meadows, Winnemucca,
Battle Mountain, Carlin, Elko, and Wells

In the twenty-two years between the saga of the Donner Party in 1846 and the building of the Central Pacific Railroad (CPRR) in 1868, tens of thousands of emigrants made the tedious trek down the Humboldt River and across of Forty-Mile Desert. A few settlers took land in the river bottom, and prospectors probed the adjacent mountains for precious metals, but no substantial settlements appeared in this corridor before 1868.

Stephen Ambrose, in his book *Nothing Like It in the World*, describes the pressures and haste under which the Big Four capitalists and the workmen on the line spanned the mountains and deserts of the West. Chinese laborers usually did the toughest and most menial jobs. Anglo–Americans shared some of their toil but usually had easier tasks. The crew boss for railroad construction was Charles Crocker.

It took four years for the CPRR to lay its tracks from Sacramento to Reno—a distance of 130 miles—because of the Sierra barrier. The CPRR laid out the town of Reno and sold lots on May 9, 1868.

From that point to the linkup with the Union Pacific at Promontory, Utah, the topography was easier but more arid and challenging in other ways. Within two months of passing Reno, the crews had reached the "big bend" of the Truckee River, where the stream turns sharply northward to its destination at Pyramid Lake. At this site, Crocker established another station and the town of Wadsworth.

Beyond that point, where the railroad line departed the Truckee River, he tried to lay a mile of track each day despite shortages of essential equipment and supplies. Along the next

250 miles of the Forty-Mile Desert and the Humboldt River, the Central Pacific established five stations in wide places with possibility for commercial development. The most promising of these were at the Big Meadows, Winnemucca, Argenta, Elko, and Wells. Towns sprouted there like exotic, imported seedlings.

THE BIG MEADOWS (LOVELOCK), PART ONE

After the Central Pacific railroad surveyors had advanced northeast beyond the Forty-Mile Desert and the brackish waters of the Humboldt Sink, they reached the "Big Meadows," a natural pastureland where the westbound emigrants of the 1840s had rested their animals before embarking on the desperate lunge toward the streams flowing down from the Sierra Nevada. This place already had a few settlers in 1868, including George Lovelock, an Englishman who had claimed land there in 1862. He was sufficiently established six years later to encourage the CPRR to build a station on his property. The nearby Trinity and Humboldt Mountain ranges attracted enough miners, cattlemen, and hay ranchers to sustain a few business establishments and a school. This was the nucleus for a town 93 miles northeast of Reno. Dozens of families—some of them immigrants from northern Europe—worked to divert the precious flow of the river into ditches and onto fields. By the 1870s, this broad valley had become one of the prime hay producers and pasturelands in the state.

WINNEMUCCA, PART ONE

About 70 miles northeast of the Big Meadows, Crocker selected another wide place, originally called Frenchman's Ford, for a Central Pacific station. He renamed this site for a legendary Paiute chief. At this point, the main channel of the Humboldt River receives a seasonal, supplementary flow from one of its main tributaries, the Little Humboldt, which tumbles down from the eastern side of Santa Rosa Mountains near the Oregon border.

Before it reaches the main channel, the Little Humboldt passes through a broad, lush valley, named by its earliest settlers "Paradise." Even now, visitors who arrive after crossing miles of parched and barren valleys are quick to endorse this nomenclature. Paradise Valley was admired for its pastureland possibilities at least five years before the railroad construction crews reached Winnemucca. Paradise has been a favorite venue for cowboys and sheepherders for 150 years.

The Central Pacific began regular railroad service through Winnemucca in the autumn of 1868. Local newspaper advertising boasted that a passenger could leave Sacramento at 6:00 AM, reach Reno at 4:14 PM, and arrive in Winnemucca at 3:20 AM. The eleven hours or so between the Truckee Meadows and Winnemucca (about 160 miles) seemed to be breakneck speed to the experienced traveler of that era.

Winnemucca quickly became an important commercial transfer point. There was no better place for moving people, livestock, and freight between the railroad and eastern Oregon. By the standards of the western mining frontier, Winnemucca's commercial development was slow. The population in 1870, according to the U.S. census, was 290, while that of the county seat in Unionville was 470. Ten years later, the situation was reversed: Winnemucca had 763 residents; Unionville had 398. By popular demand, the legislature moved the Humboldt county seat from its original site to Winnemucca in 1873.

ARGENTA AND BATTLE MOUNTAIN, PART ONE

As the crews of the Central Pacific pushed eastward in the spring of 1869, Crocker's scouts identified a place 65 miles beyond Winnemucca for their next town, near the so-called Argenta Mountains, a name chosen from the Spanish word for silver. This time, however, the earliest settlers made a different choice, relocating about 12 miles downstream at a place they called Battle Mountain despite the fact that it was on rather level terrain. It was near a promontory where an earlier fight with Indians had occurred and was thought to be closer to promising mines. Ambiguity about the name lingered, as the voting precinct and mining district were for many years still called Argenta.

The site of Battle Mountain had the advantage of being directly north of Austin where the Reese River trickles (or, at rare times, floods) into the Humboldt River. Unlike Winnemucca to the west and Elko to the east, this place was not laid out by Crocker. It began more or less spontaneously in 1870, linked to Austin,

93 miles to the south, by a stage line. Both towns were within the boundaries of Lander County, now greatly reduced since its creation.

During the 1870s, investors wrestled with the idea of building a branch line between the two towns. Technical and financial problems delayed a link for most of the decade, but eventually the wealthy financier, Anson Phelps Stokes, came to the rescue and completed the Nevada Central Railroad. Most of the project was finished in a rush in the winter of 1879–80 to take advantage of a bond authorized earlier by the Nevada legislature. The first trains needed about eight hours (at 11 miles per hour) to travel between the two towns, but the railroad survived—with many interruptions—until 1938.

Stokes gained his most enduring fame in central Nevada not for his railroad or his castle west of Austin. He also sent a young attorney named Tasker L. Oddie from the East to Nevada to look after his interests. This enterprising man became interested in mining at Tonopah, which led to his election as governor and two terms as United States senator.

THREE MORE RAILROAD TOWNS: CARLIN, ELKO, AND WELLS

Advanced teams from the Central Pacific laid out both Carlin and Elko during the last weeks of 1868. The former was selected for a roundhouse and maintenance yards. This decision may have been influenced by the fact that the valley to the north pointed toward the promising mining district of Tuscarora (40 miles away), and the valley to the south offered easy passage to Eureka (92 miles distant). Carlin was designated as a division point, but it was not able to compete with Elko, 25 miles east, as a magnet for settlers.

The community of Wells, 50 miles east of Elko, had a different genesis. Originally known as Humboldt Wells, it had been a favorite resting place for westbound wagon trains in the 1840s and 1850s after they had crossed the barren salt flats of Utah. The flowing springs offered plenty of fresh water for emigrants and their animals. The Central Pacific chose it as a town site in 1868 for the same reason.

During the winter of 1868–69, as CP construction crews rushed to connect with the Union Pacific at Promontory, Utah

Territory, Elko became the commercial and political hub of north-eastern Nevada. Situated about 300 miles east of Carson City and about 200 miles west of Salt Lake City, it was destined from the beginning to be a prominent place on the maps of the Great Basin.

Rich silver mines had been discovered in the White Pine Mountains nearly 200 miles to the south. By 1869, prospectors drawn to this remote magnet could travel part of the distance in a railroad car rather than on foot or by crude wagon.

One such traveler was Franklin A. Buck, a New Englander who had followed the gold rush to California in 1849 and had many disappointments. Twenty years later, he was one of the first to ride the newly installed rails from Sacramento to Elko, sending a lively verbal description of his voyage to relatives in the East. He enjoyed the luxury of the railroad cars (built in Massachusetts, he noted) but was not favorably impressed with the terrain of the Humboldt—"a vast plain of sand, sagebrush and alkali." His comments were later gathered into a book, *A Yankee Trader in the Goldrush*, which chronicled many episodes in his journey though eastern Nevada.

When Buck wrote his letter from the infant town of Elko on April 9, 1869, connection with the Union Pacific had not yet been made, but trains had been arriving regularly from California for several weeks. Linkage of the two railroads followed about a month later.

By the time Buck visited, Elko was almost an established town. Lots had been sold at auction and the legislature in Carson City had made it the county seat. "There are probably 150 houses or tents and one or two thousand people here," he wrote. "Prices are moderate.... The stores contain every article you can call for. We have fresh salmon and green peas from California every day."

The town and the county of the same name were quite stable through the 1870s, unlike most silver-mining camps. In the census of 1880, Elko County had 5,716 residents—second only to Storey County (Virginia City and Gold Hill) in population.

Not only did Elko become the distribution point for a vast region but the adjacent valleys and mountains provided excellent forage for cattle and sheep. Stockmen, who put their animals on the open range to "fatten them up," usually drove them into Elko for shipment to eastern or California markets. Elko was a cowboy town from the beginning.

NEVADA'S SECOND GOVERNOR, "BROADHORNS" BRADLEY

One of the early cowmen who grazed his herds was Lewis R. Bradley. He had driven longhorns into the western part of Nevada Territory as early as 1862, then gradually shifted his operations eastward in the Basin, settling in Elko and entering politics soon after the town was born.

"Broadhorns" Bradley, as he was affectionately called, was twice elected governor (1870 and 1874) and made his mark on the state in two memorable ways. First, he tried to reform Nevada's lax rules on the taxation of mines. He failed, and this effort cost him a third term in 1878. Second, he persuaded the 1873 session of the legislature to establish an "Academic or Preparatory" department of a state university in Elko.

One fact that aroused the governor and the legislature in 1873 was a provision in the federal land-grant law that allowed the state to establish a university that would offer instruction in agriculture and the mechanic arts within ten years of admission to the Union. Nevada risked losing 90,000 acres of federal land entitlement if it did not act by 1874.

The earliest state law authorizing a university did not specify a location, but it insisted that the host community must provide at least 20 acres and a building worth at least $10,000 to the new academy. Governor Bradley persuaded the Board of Regents that Elko was the place, and Central Pacific donated the necessary acres.

This seemed to be a major achievement, but it proved to be a questionable asset. Although the Central Pacific donated a tract of land and local citizens raised the required amount of money, Elko was less than five years old when the experiment began. It had no pool of potential students able and willing to attend.

A handsome wooden classroom building arose and even a dormitory. But the expected number of scholars never arrived. The maximum enrollment was about thirty. The Elko phase of Nevada's university experiment ended in 1885, when the legislature voted to move the fledgling college to Reno. Elko had to wait another seventy-five years to host a viable college.

THE CPRR: NOURISHING BUT ABUSIVE PARENT

Railroads have been intertwined with the history of the towns, ranches, and mines along the Humboldt corridor for more than 150 years. The Central Pacific was the father and mother of Lovelock, Winnemucca, Battle Mountain, Elko, and Wells. It gave them birth and nourished them in the beginning. Its freight hauling services enabled them to get supplies and to ship livestock to distant markets.

But the CPRR also became an abusive parent with the gouging rates it charged for incoming goods. Railroad managers set much higher freight-hauling rates for interior towns than it imposed on California customers. The company charged $1,200 to haul a carload of clothing from New York to Oakland, but the same carload, if dropped off at Winnemucca, would cost $1,616. This was the so-called "back-haul rate," as if the cargo had gone all the way to the San Francisco bay area and back, although it would actually have been unloaded at Winnemucca.

The railroad could impose such charges with impunity because it had no competition for its inland services, while a seaport such as San Francisco had another option. A Nevada Congressman, Rollin Daggett, made this case in the House of Representatives in 1879. His impassioned words brought no immediate relief and led to his defeat when he sought re-election in 1880 as railroad bosses gave financial support to his opponent.

Central Pacific agents in Nevada could easily manipulate the election of U.S. senators, since at that time senators were elected by the legislature. State assemblymen and senators repeatedly chose John P. Jones, who had been a successful Comstock Mining superintendent, and William M. Stewart, a Carson City attorney who had represented the mining companies. Both were longtime friends of the railroad corporations and well compensated for their services. But to the citizens living along the Humboldt corridor they were not friends.

Another matter complicated the relationship between the railroad parent and those it pretended to serve. When Congress enacted legislation that authorized railroad construction in the 1860s, it made a generous grant of land to the builders. Alternate sections in each township in a 20-mile swath on both sides of the railroad were meant to encourage settlement and development—the so-called "checkerboard lands." This policy worked well in the midsection of the United States where rain was more plentiful, but in arid Nevada it simply gave the Central Pacific (and its successor companies) a vast resource for future profits. In practice, it meant that the Central Pacific had much control over the squares in the checkerboard that it did not own, because railroad agents could theoretically restrict access by using trespass laws.

The State of Nevada was originally entitled to 3.9 million acres in land grants from the federal government. The plan assumed this allotment could be sold to finance public schools. The problem was that most of the designated parcels were useless desert acres with no possibility of cultivation. And some of the most usable lands along the Humboldt had already been granted to the CP.

In 1880, the state made a bargain, agreeing to yield half of its school-land entitlement back to the federal government in exchange for the right to choose and sell half—or 2 million acres—at locations where potential settlers might be willing to buy. The prevailing logic in the state government was that if settlers could choose their own acres, rather than follow a federal checkerboard, they would get better cultivation possibilities. But in the final analysis, much of the acreage went to livestock owners who selected parcels near water resources, convenient for grazing their animals.

When the dust had settled on Nevada's land-management policies in the late nineteenth century, the Central Pacific owned about 5 million acres; the State of Nevada about 2.7 million. Most usable land available to the state was claimed and sold quickly at bargain prices. Land speculators were "Johnny-on-the-spot" to snap up the most promising parcels near available water sources. Odds were against the small farmers and ranchers. Further, thousands of families brought skills and practices that had served them well in the East and Middle West; here, most of them failed.

During the last decade of the nineteenth century, the CPRR fell into a financial crisis that threatened the company with receivership. In spite of its land and railroad assets, poor financial management put the once celebrated company in peril. The

individual who devised the solution—the takeover of the Central Pacific by the Southern Pacific (SPRR) in 1899—was Collis P.
Huntington, a skillful entrepreneur based in southern California.
Several improvements in the original line followed in the early
twentieth century.

CHAPTER FOUR

Nineteenth-Century Towns of the Middle Corridor

Belmont, Pahranagat, Hamilton,
Pioche, Panaca, and Eureka

The Central Pacific planned and planted most of its towns along the Humboldt corridor systematically, quickly, and sequentially from west to east.

No such pattern guided the settlements across the central corridor. Prospectors reaching out from Virginia City and Austin reported their discoveries randomly, and local newspapers scattered the rumors like gusts of wind in the springtime. Towns were sprinkled in reckless profusion among the mountain ranges.

One of the earliest, after Austin, was at Ione in the Shoshone Mountains in 1863. A few months later, when the territorial legislature heard rumors that more than a thousand people were living there, it created Nye County (1864), covering the entire southeastern corner of its jurisdiction. The lawmakers named the new county for the popular governor, James W. Nye. Ione never prospered, but three years later, following the opening of the Belmont District 50 miles to the southeast, a new option was available. Belmont lingered as a county seat for three decades before its torch passed to Tonopah.

BELMONT

Belmont sits on a gentle slope at an elevation of 7,400 feet in the Toquima Range. It has been called a stepchild of Austin, 90 miles to the north, because most of the early exploration and commercial support came from there. Hundreds of mining claims were staked out in the nearby mountains in 1866 and 1867. At least five stamp mills, similar to those used in Virginia City to crush ores, offered their services to the local mining companies. The legislature then voted to move the county seat here from Ione.

After about two years, this promising start was interrupted by rumors of a fabulous new strike in the White Pine Mountains (and we will soon consider Hamilton and Treasure City) about 100 miles to the northeast. But in the mid-1870s, after the excitement in other mining districts had cooled, Belmont got a second chance. During that brief revival, Nye County's officers had enough confidence to build an attractive court house, faced with red brick. A dozen surviving photographs suggest an abundance of civic pride in the building.

Census data show that such confidence was premature. While there may have been as many as 2,000 people in the vicinity during the prosperous years, at no point between 1870 and 1900 did the U.S. census find more than 2,000 residents in all of Nye County nor more than 300 in Belmont.

Because its productive and prosperous periods were so brief, Belmont never had the advantages of a railroad, although the possibility of a connection to Austin was occasionally mentioned in the newspapers. Its mining production, according to the most reliable reports, never reached as much as a half-million dollars a year after 1873. Nearly all the precious metal taken from its mines was produced before 1873.

The most famous individual associated with Belmont was the legendary Jim Butler, who discovered Tonopah in 1900. A jack-of-all-trades, he had a ranch in Monitor Valley, friends in Austin, and the basic skills of a part-time prospector. He became Nye County's district attorney in the late 1890s without any formal training in the law. The story of his discovery of Tonopah has often been told.

Belmont lost its status as the county seat to Tonopah in 1905. The shell of the Belmont courthouse was still standing early in the twenty-first century, more than 125 years after the mines and mills fell dormant and is the main attraction of a remote historic park.

Pahranagat

In 1864, when the Territory of Nevada received statehood, its eastern boundary was defined by law at 115 degrees of longitude. But longitude lines were difficult to define on the ground then and required careful surveys.

There was no doubt that the White Pine region was in Nevada, not in Utah Territory. But when prospectors discovered silver-bearing rocks near Irish Mountain west of the Pahranagat Valley in 1865–66, and scores of would-be miners rushed there, a question of jurisdiction arose. Rumors of a potential bonanza soon reached Carson City, Salt Lake City, and even Washington, D.C., where Nevada's congressional delegation managed to enact a law extending the new state's jurisdiction one degree of longitude eastward to include the Pahranagat region. Nevada's congressional representative at the time was Delos Ashley of Austin, who played an important role in moving the state line.

An Act of Congress in 1867 also provided for the expansion of Nevada southward from the 37th parallel—the original southern boundary—to the Colorado River and the 35th parallel, based on the theory that this waterway was navigable far upstream from its outlet in the Gulf of California. Thus the Las Vegas region, which had previously been part of Arizona Territory, became an adopted child of Nevada, without the consent or knowledge of people living or trading there. Mormon missionaries built a fort and cultivated a few acres at Las Vegas between 1855 and 1858, but their experiment had failed. In the middle 1860s, Octavius D. Gass of Arizona Territory had taken possession and cultivated lands around the oasis. Gass believed his property was in Arizona Territory when news about the boundary change reached him. In fact, he was a member of the Arizona territorial legislature at the time.

The Gold Hill Daily News, one of the leading Nevada newspapers of the time, speculated wildly on June 7, 1865, that the Colorado River was navigable for 600 miles upstream from its mouth. The News anticipated great benefit for the southern part of Nevada as well as to Arizona and Utah territories.

The new government in Carson City had no clear idea of what it had inherited by the annexation, but lawmakers felt a sense of urgency to bring these remote sections into the Nevada fold. In 1866, the legislature established Lincoln County, embracing about 17,000 square miles in the southeastern corner of the state. An oasis called Crystal Springs in the Pahranagat Valley was designated as the county seat because it seemed to be the best site for a town near the promising mines at Irish Mountain.

In the spring of 1866, the state's first elected governor, Henry G. Blasdel, traveled from Carson City to Pahranagat and back, a round trip of about 800 miles, to inspect the mines and organize a local government. His trip was chronicled in the pages of Austin's *Reese River Reveille*. His contingent of explorers had no reliable maps and passed through "death barren" by an untested route. One man died when they ran short of water, and hopes were dashed when they did not find enough citizens in the Pahranagat area to constitute a county government.

The enthusiasm for Irish Mountain riches cooled within two years, and only the shell of a county government remained. In 1867, the legislature tried again to create a viable county and designated Hiko, a village where a small stamp mill had been built, as the county seat.

The Irish Mountain mines fizzled more rapidly than those of the White Pine district. In 1868, the U.S government's Commissioner for Mines estimated that about $933,000 had been invested in Pahranagat ventures, but only about $20,000 in ore had been extracted.

In the summer of 1871, a news item in Virginia City's *Daily Territorial Enterprise* summarized how remote this region was from the center of Nevada's political affairs. It offered advice (which originated with "a Pioche correspondent of the *Enterprise*") on the best way to proceed to Arizona Territory. "Glowing reports" had been received from there about mining possibilities. The article recommended that a traveler proceed to Belmont and "thence to Pahranagat Valley; then down the valley to its terminus (good feed); thence to the Muddy (two days); thence to Las Vegas Ranch, where feed must be purchased; thence to Fort Mohave, on the Colorado...." (*Daily Territorial Enterprise*, August 12, 1871, 2:1.)

HAMILTON AND TREASURE CITY, 1869–87

The most exciting gold-silver discovery of the 1860s along the central corridor occurred nearly 250 miles east of Virginia City in the White Pine Mountains. In rugged terrain at an elevation between 8,000 and 9,000 feet, prospectors from Austin identified silver ore as early as 1865. Word of the discovery spread rapidly, but the great distances from any existing settlements and the extreme elevation delayed development for nearly three years.

When the "rush to White Pine" began in 1868–69, local boosters and distant journalists anticipated great riches would be mined near the surface of these often-frosty highlands. Swarming crowds of prospectors, businessmen, and camp followers ascended the canyons and slopes to start several towns, the largest of which were Hamilton and Treasure City. Nowhere else in the inland West did such extravagant claims attract more suckers to such high terrain.

Promoters and local historians of later years made wild estimates of the numbers of people who came. The reports that 10,000 reached the district may have been exaggerated, but the official census of 1870 showed nearly 7,000 residents (though one is tempted to question the census figures).

One of those who arrived in the spring of 1869 was Franklin Buck, whom we met earlier in Elko. When Buck saw some of the White Pine rock samples in San Francisco in 1869, he believed the reports that it contained ore worth $20,000 per ton.

Buck came to Treasure City in April 1869, finding a bustling camp of prospectors and merchants already there. "The street is crowded with teams and pack mules and the saloons and stores filled with men," he wrote. "Petticoats are very scarce,… A great many of the buildings are of stone. Here is a telegraph line, a daily paper, good hotels, magnificent whisky saloons, stores filled with everything you can call for and it has all been done since January 1, 1869…" (Buck, 221). "I have not found a place to pitch our tent yet. The weather has been so bad, and I have been busy looking at the mines"(Buck, 223).

Investors from San Francisco, the East, and London poured money into mining stocks at an astounding rate. Historian Russell R. Elliott has traced as much as $246 million that may have been invested in the early years. Official records show that the White Pine mines yielded about $7 million in precious metals between 1868 and 1873. By comparison, the Comstock Lode was producing upwards of $40 million during the same period. In the next few years, the mines of Virginia City and Gold Hill went on to extract hundreds of millions more from the Big Bonanza in the mid-1870s, while Hamilton and Treasure City slipped into oblivion. Yet while it lived, the White Pine district was home to three newspapers.

The brief bonanza left a political legacy. The legislature in Carson City created White Pine County during its 1869 session and designated Hamilton as the seat of local government. Local political leaders built a courthouse, but when it was destroyed by fire, the county seat was removed to Ely in 1887. Some of the stone walls of Hamilton's commercial buildings stood until the middle of the twentieth century but eventually succumbed to weather and vandalism.

AN ODD COUPLE: BONANZA DAYS IN PIOCHE AND MORMON SETTLERS IN PANACA

In the late 1860s, the tumultuous mining rush and a well-planned Mormon communal frontier confronted each other in one of those places where the crumbled geology of the Great Basin puts rugged mountains and lush little valleys side by side.

Meadow Valley is a small northern tributary of the Colorado River. Its pastures and fertile soil attracted the expanding Mormon empire from Utah. But the mountains immediately to the north also became a magnet for the mining frontier expanding from Belmont and Hamilton, as well as from Utah. Panaca and Pioche were 10 miles apart but topographically and socially quite different.

Pioche is crowded into a narrow canyon facing north with a magnificent view into a vast valley tinted with the purple and gray of high-desert shrubs. Its vista includes the Snake Range, where many decades later Nevada's environmentalists managed to establish the Great Basin National Park.

Panaca is oriented in a different direction—eastward toward Utah. The Latter-day Saints began building a communal settlement there in 1864, laying out street blocks and irrigation ditches and planting gardens.

News of the silver discovery 10 miles north spread in all directions. From St. George, Utah, and Salt Lake City; from Hiko and Virginia City; and even from California, came prospectors, investors, and merchants. They congregated near the so-called Panaca claims in turbulent Pioche. Here, a sequel to the drama at Hamilton played out but at a lower elevation and in close proximity to an outpost of the Mormon empire.

The first signs of interest came from southern Utah, even though Mormon leaders were suspicious of mining activity unless it was conducted by their own flock. They usually discouraged the search for gold and silver, remembering that earlier rushes had drawn motley, raucous crowds to California and northern Nevada, a result incompatible with their visions of a peaceful Zion. But when a silver lode was known to exist near their villages, some of the Latter-day Saints wanted to claim it.

Erastus Snow and other leaders of the southern Utah Mormon mission were ambivalent about the close relationship between church members in Panaca and the "gentiles" (as all non-Mormons were called) of the mining camps. (An excellent, more recent summary of the competition among the miners of Pioche, the Mormons of Panaca, and the Native Americans is available in the research of W. Paul Reeve).

BOOM AND BUST IN PIOCHE

When news of the "Meadow Valley" discovery spread in Utah Territory, it caught the attention of an eclectic entrepreneur from Salt Lake City—Patrick Connor. As the leader of the federal army that had arrived in Salt Lake City after the so-called "Mormon War" of 1857, he participated in the search for precious metals throughout the far West. He and some of his troops explored the Meadow Valley region as early as 1864, and he returned to Pioche as the town was being laid out in 1870.

Connor became an active participant in its business life during the boom years. He visited the town several times, invested in the mines, and promoted a railroad that would have connected Pioche to Salt Lake City—if it had been built. But like most investors, he became discouraged in the middle 1870s and sold his interests.

Two competitors of General Connor were the partners William Raymond and John Ely, who had tried to process the ores in the Pahranagat district. Failing there, they relocated their milling operation near Panaca at a place they named Bullionville. It provided a generous supply of water, and a number of nearby Mormon men could be hired to haul the ore down from Pioche and to mill it.

Their mining property became the famous Raymond & Ely (R & E) Mine, the richest in Pioche. It produced about sixty percent of the precious metals that came from the district during the bonanza years of 1870–75. Like successful producers elsewhere, they had to litigate in court to protect their claims and found it necessary to hire gunmen to hold back claim-jumpers.

In the meantime, a San Francisco capitalist also learned of the prospects. Francois L. A. Pioche sent his agents to stake claims and lay out a town in the canyon. This group became a leader in the race to exploit the ores. This French-born entrepreneur had many investments in California and was one of the Bay Area's most famous plutocrats.

At the beginning of 1871, news of the Pioche mining boom stirred excitement even in Virginia City. The *Daily Territorial Enterprise* reported that men were leaving "almost daily for that camp and vicinity," where the mines had a "good solid foundation" (DTE, January 6, 1871, 2:3).

Two years later, when the boom was near its peak, the perspective was different. The local paper reported: "Crime is rampant in Pioche. Law-defyers, of high and low degree, emboldened by immunity from arrest and punishment for former transgressions, are seemingly more vicious and audacious with each returning day. The officers of the law seem almost powerless in their efforts to give good citizens peace and security under the law; and when honest men come together the first topic of conversation is the deplorable state of public morals." The frenzy declined after a year or two, but the public cemetery of Pioche in the twenty-first century still has a row of grave mounds called Boot Hill to remind the town and its tourists of its rowdy beginning.

The mines of Pioche yielded more than $15 million in gold and silver in fewer than five years during the 1870s—much more than Austin, Belmont, and Hamilton. For a few months, it seemed to be the second-richest camp in Nevada—a rival of the fabled Comstock Lode. But its miners encountered too much water at the 1,200-foot level underground, and the pumps of the 1870s could not lift it to the surface. When the price of silver fell sharply in 1873, the town declined. By 1877, it was already deeply into "borrasca" in the vocabulary of the mining fraternity—out of ore and out of luck.

Pioche survived because it was the Lincoln County seat after 1871 and the commercial center for the vast rangeland to the north where cattle and sheep could be grazed and driven to a railroad loading point in Utah. Franklin Buck arrived in Pioche in 1870. "I have found one mining camp at the start," he wrote hopefully. He built a comfortable home, invested in livestock, and operated a lumber business. His letters to relatives in New England chronicle a period of exuberant marketing and prospecting for a few years and then the gradual decline. In 1878, Buck sent a poignant swan song to his relatives. "This town has completely gone in. Petered out. Everybody is leaving who can."

Pioche then settled into a long slumber, a Rip Van Winkle sleep that lasted more than twenty years. The hastily built wooden homes of the 1870s weathered poorly during the dry summers and cold, windy winters. Business buildings on Main Street, constructed mainly from native quartzite, had a longer life span, but they too crumbled over the decades because there was no mortar other than mud holding the stone walls together.

Pioche was an unplanned town: its narrow streets twisted along the canyon walls in an irregular tangle. Such a town, with its rich ores and rowdy ways, presented a challenge to the Mormon ideal of a quiet, self-sustaining village on the fringe of Zion. The relationship between Pioche and its Latter-day Saints (LDS) neighbors in Panaca offer lessons in establishing tolerance between two distinct cultures.

MORMONS IN PANACA

The small oasis named Panaca was known to the Latter-day Saints of Utah Territory as early as 1857. At the time, troops were approaching Salt Lake City to enforce federal law, which President James Buchanan believed church leaders were defying. A group of LDS scouts searched a broad expanse of the central Great Basin for a "Place of Refuge," in case it should become necessary for church leaders and their families to abandon Salt Lake City. A small contingent of explorers dug irrigation ditches and planted crops in Meadow Valley before the so-called "Utah War" ended (Brooks, "A Place of Refuge").

The town of Panaca was established in the same place six years later in the spring of 1864, mostly by settlers from the St. George, Utah, area, encouraged by the Cotton Mission of the Mormon Church. The town replicated the traditional pattern of the LDS villages in Utah Territory, with the town divided into a compass-oriented gridiron and wide streets lined with Lombardy poplars. Each square embraced 6.4 acres, divided into four 1.6-acre lots assigned to individual families by lottery.

A central quadrangle intended for community purposes specified where the church and schools would eventually be built. Near this center, were spaces intended for stores and other commercial services. Irrigation ditches distributed water from the nearby spring according to a shared, communal plan. Panaca, unlike the mining towns, was not settled quickly or in a rush. Once Mormon leaders identified a spot where colonization was possible, settlers began to build houses of adobe, according to a plan well tested in Utah. In Panaca, this started in 1864 and required years of labor. The residents had the support of the church in planting their gardens and introducing livestock. A commercial row of buildings emerged along Third Street, the main east-west arterial. The leading business venture here, as in all Mormon towns, was Zion's Cooperative Mercantile Institution (ZCMI), a church-owned general store that made its goods available to Mormons and non-Mormons alike.

Soon after Panaca's first growing season, its farmers had markets for their produce in the towns of the Cotton Mission of St. George and in the Pahranagat area. Four or five years later, the prospectors and miners of Pioche provided a much closer, more lucrative market.

As Pioche became the leading eastern Nevada mining locale of the 1870s, Panaca's farmers and merchants prospered as few other Mormon towns of the southern Great Basin did. The milling activity at Bullionville at the northern edge of Meadow Valley 2 miles north of Panaca made the bond between the two towns unusually strong. Bullionville survived for only a few years. When the mining boom at Pioche receded, the mill closed and the moveable property was hauled off or decayed in place, but Panaca's industrious families continued to tend their farms.

When the definitive boundary-line survey between Nevada and Utah Territory in 1871 showed Panaca and other Mormon communities farther south to be in Nevada, most LDS members living in the Moapa and Virgin valleys moved to Utah. But several families in Panaca decided to stay. Their profitable arrangements with the Pioche miners and Bullionville millers seemed preferable. Even after the Pioche boom fizzled, Panacans made an acceptable living with their gardens and livestock. The 1900 U.S. census counted 339 residents in Panaca.

Thus Nevada has inherited a small sample of Utah's nineteenth-century communal culture, featuring wide streets, rows of carefully planted poplar trees, and signs of old irrigation ditches that remained into the twenty-first century.

The ward house was the nerve center of community life, the religious and social bond that church life provided. In no other place in Nevada was such a community-oriented structure so prominent except in the LDS villages established later. In most other Nevada communities, whose popular ideals arose from precious-metal mining, railroading, and livestock herding, a strong bias against Mormon beliefs prevailed. This was probably due in part, because many elders of the church practiced polygamy in Utah. But in both Pioche and Panaca, the tension was muted, for the towns were economically interdependent and sufficiently distinct.

Panaca and Pioche made a classic Odd Couple. Residents of each town ridiculed and scorned the lifestyles of the other. Pioche was rowdy and haphazard; Panaca was tidy and quiet, dedicated to building the new Zion. But they were mostly tolerant neighbors, since Pioche miners were regular consumer of Panaca's farm products. When a countywide high school was established in 1909, it was located in the central square in Panaca, which the Mormon settlers had established forty-five years earlier.

In the annals of Nevada history, Pioche became most famous for a scandal involving its courthouse. This structure was built in 1871–72 after the county seat had been transferred from Hiko. During the early fever of the mining boom, the county commissioner authorized construction of a substantial but modest building, mainly from the local quartzite.

To build this new symbol of the county's prosperity, the commissioners borrowed money issued as "scrip"—an informal promise to pay in the future. Before the building was finished, these same officers authorized extravagant payments to the sheriff, presumably to collect taxes. They then devised a scheme to issue bonds to construct a branch railroad line extending 200 miles north to connect with the Central Pacific at Palisade.

This last scheme won the approval of both houses of the state legislature in 1873, but Governor Bradley vetoed the bill. Nevertheless, the county had already incurred the most burdensome debt in the history of local government in Nevada. In 1873, the commissioners issued $181,000 in bonds to consolidate all its obligations and sold them at ten percent interest.

The collapse of the mines was already underway before this pattern of scheming and borrowing had run its course. As the silver output decreased, debt continued to grow until it reached an estimated $650,000 in 1907. The state legislature tried to intervene several times before a solution finally presented itself in 1909. At that point, Clark County was established from the southern portion of Lincoln, following completion of a rail line between Salt Lake and Los Angeles.

The establishment of Las Vegas and the emergence of a broader property tax base finally enabled the county government to dispose of this obligation after thirty years. Newly created Clark County was obliged to assume a large portion of the "courthouse debt."

EUREKA

One mining camp escaped the downward spiral that left so many ghost towns across Nevada's landscape. Eureka, located about 45 miles northwest of Hamilton and nearly 200 miles from Pioche, had a less spectacular story but enjoyed its early prosperity longer than any other town in the North-Center. It then languished for almost a century before it found new life during the gold bonanza of the twentieth century, having retained much of its cultural infrastructure.

The Eureka Mining District was formed in September 1864, about six weeks before President Lincoln signed the proclamation admitting Nevada to the Union as the thirty-sixth state, but exploitation of the ores only began several years later. The first year of substantial production was 1871, when more than $2 million was reported. Although Eureka's productivity was not comparable to that of the Comstock Lode, it had a longer life. During their first twenty years, Eureka's mines yielded more than $45 million.

In 1873, the state legislature detached another slice of Lander County to create Eureka County. Unlike other newly established counties of the era, Eureka did not rush into an expensive building project for its public offices. Instead, it adapted a former skating rink for county government business, a venue that served for several years. With deliberate care, the early Eureka commissioners planned several years before settling on a two-story, red brick building with a tasteful interior accented by an ornate courtroom. When the county commissioners accepted the structure in 1879, the total cost was said to have been $38,000. (A vault and other additions later added to this figure). Such frugality was not typical of most local Nevada governments Nevada.

Across the main street, investors built an elegant opera house. It opened a year after the courthouse, which it complemented with a handsome red brick facade, and became the main community gathering place, with a dance hall and later a movie theater. After a period of neglect and deterioration, the county government acquired the building in the 1990s and restored it beyond its original elegance, using some of the tax revenue from the twentieth-century gold mines.

A view of Eureka's early prosperity was recorded in a booklet entitled *Eureka and Its Resources*, published in 1879 by Lambert Molinelli, an Italian immigrant and jack-of-all-trades who served briefly as county recorder. The booklet appeared approximately at the midpoint of the town's mining boom and about when the courthouse and opera house were being completed and is a summary of regional commercial and industrial activity.

Eureka's ores, like those of most other mining districts, had their main values in silver. Early developers were able to design smelters to recover substantial amounts of gold and lead as by-products. In its earliest years, Eureka became center for the smelting as well as mining and endured the consequences of heavy smoke often trapped in the confines of its narrow canyon. Nearby juniper and pinyon forests provided wood for the charcoal ovens that produced "coke" for the smelters.

Nevada mining towns usually attracted immigrants willing to work in the mines and related industries for meager wages. Thus Eureka became a magnet for foreign-born laborers in the late 1870s. Nearly sixty percent of the 7,086 people counted in Eureka during the 1880 census had been born outside the United States.

One of the largest groups was the Italians, many of whom worked in the mountains cutting and hauling wood for the charcoal. They were members of the "carbonari" of their native land, a proud fraternity that resembled a modern industrial union in representing the interests of their members. The most violent confrontation in early Nevada mining history occurred in 1879, when middlemen who were buying charcoal for the smelters tried to reduce the prices they were paying to the carbonari. When the workers acted to prevent coke delivery, the sheriff formed a posse, and the ensuing fight resulted in the murder of five Italian workers. Twenty more men were wounded or locked in jail. Local authorities stalled any serious investigation, and no one was ever punished. The "Fish Creek Massacre" became a stain on Eureka's history and the subject of several later investigations.

Eureka had several newspapers during the bonanza years, the first published as early as July 1870; the *Eureka Sentinel* was printed there for ninety years (until 1960), when it was absorbed into a central-Nevada consortium and published from Tonopah. The Sentinel building was adapted to serve as the county museum.

One of the artifacts of the nineteenth century that did not survive into the contemporary era was the Eureka and Palisade Railroad, built in 1874–75 to connect the community with the Central Pacific line 85 miles north. For more than a decade, it was one of the most successful short-lines in the state, recording a profit in most years. During the bonanza era, the local newspaper suggested the E&P might be extended as far south as Pioche and from there perhaps to the Colorado River—a distance of nearly 300 miles. As the town fell on hard times, the E&P lost its glitter and went into bankruptcy in 1893. Yet it endured a series of floods and managed intermittent service between Eureka and the Humboldt River until 1938.

When the silver mining business crashed in the 1880s, Eureka coasted to a soft landing; the falloff in production was slower than the busts in most other camps. It was an anomaly among the nineteenth-century boomtowns, surviving into the twenty-first century with many of the most admirable buildings intact. Its short main street offers the best-preserved example of nineteenth-century mining town opulence in the North-Center.

In addition to the opera house, the ornate courthouse received an extensive and careful restoration in the late twentieth century and is still in use nearly 140 years after it was built. The high-ceiling center aisle of the ground floor, the ornate wooden staircase to the second floor, and the elegant courtroom testify both to the prosperity of the original boom and the continuing affection of Eureka's citizens for the early days. The bonanza of the late twentieth century has enabled them to restore their public buildings with good taste, rather than to tear them down. As mentioned earlier, Eureka is a special exception to the general pattern of the Nevada mining frontier.

Another enduring sample of local cultural aspirations in the late 1870s may be found in the sketches and tints of one of its residents, Walter S. Long. He produced a body of watercolors of Eureka and several other towns of the North-Center. Much of his work of that decade has been collected and organized by Michael J. Broadhead and James C. McCormick, formerly professors at the University of Nevada in Reno.

Long was a veteran of the Civil War and civil engineer who found himself in Eureka just as the boom was receding. He left a collection of more than sixty delicate, detailed images, intended for a woman whom he loved, then living in Boston. The evocative images present the region in a way that the black-and-white photographs of the day could not achieve.

Echoes from John Muir

John Muir, the renowned naturalist and founder of the Sierra Club, commented on the Nevada scene in 1879 in an article published in the *San Francisco Evening Bulletin*, which was later included in his book *Steep Trails*. "Nevada is one of the very youngest and wildest of the States," he wrote; "nevertheless it is already strewn with ruins that seem as gray and silent and time-worn as if the civilization to which they belonged had perished centuries ago. Yet, strange to say, all these ruins are results of mining efforts made within the last few years."

When Muir visited central Nevada over three summers in the late 1870s, he found at least five "dead" towns for each "live" one. His prose descriptions typify the gentle eloquence of the era. "Mining discoveries and progress, retrogression and decay, seem to have been crowded more closely against each other here than on any other portion of the globe."

Muir's insights into Nevada are like an exhibit of delicate, miniature treasures, stored in a case or a half-forgotten attic for more than a century. When rediscovered and dusted off, they surprise us with their brilliance. Writing in the town of Ward (White Pine County) in 1879, he made predictions about Nevada's unsuitability for traditional farming and industry: "...one vast desert, all sage and sand, hopelessly irredeemable, now and forever." Yet he recognized that there were places on the slopes of the mountain ranges where the industrious farmer could make a good living raising barley and alfalfa hay. He ended his essay with speculation about other possibilities for this strange land he had learned to love after three summers in its seductive embrace.

"Whether any considerable area of these sage plains will ever thus be made to blossom in grass and wheat, experience will show. But in the mean time Nevada is beautiful in her wildness, and if tillers of the soil can thus be brought to see that possibly Nature may have other uses even for rich soil besides the feeding of human beings, then will these foodless 'deserts' have taught us a fine lesson."

CHAPTER FIVE

The Politics of Conscience

*Silver Crusade, Native American Policy,
and Woman Suffrage*

Three of the most controversial political problems that excited
Nevada's widely scattered voters during the last quarter of the
nineteenth century involved (1) monetary policy (silver vs. gold
coinage); (2) policies toward Native Americans; and (3) the proposal to extend voting rights to women and African–Americans.
A fourth issue, involving land and water policies, will be discussed
in chapter 6.

SILVER CRUSADE

When the price for silver ore plummeted in the 1870s, most mining
camps across the inland West were hit hard. Prospectors and producers in western states had staked so many claims, had formed so
many districts, and had refined so much ore that when the value
of the "white metal" dropped sharply in relation to gold, it was
not merely a "great recession," it was the beginning of a "twenty-
year depression," as Nevada historians have frequently defined it.

As Nevada mines lost their luster during the 1880s, the state's
politicians and voters found a scapegoat in the U.S. government's
monetary policy and villains in Washington. In 1873, Congress had
passed a law deleting a clause that authorized the minting of new
silver coins. In the political rhetoric of the time, this "crime of '73"
became a rallying cry for westerners, who demanded the free and
unlimited coinage of silver. The congressional decision about minting silver dollars was obviously not the main cause of the West's
economic problems, but it became the protest slogan of the era.

The "silver crusade" evoked angry resentment against the
"goldbug" manipulators of monetary policy in Washington and

"the East." (Historians who study the Tea Party movement of the twenty-first century might find antecedents here.) The goldbugs were the perceived enemies of the struggling workingmen of the West. In the 1890s, when the cauldron of "free silver" came to full boil, four of the most active leaders of the movement resided and published their aspiration in the North-Center:

1. George Nixon of Winnemucca brought one the loudest and most persistent voices in favor of resuming silver coinage to his Nevada audience. He was a banker who also owned the local newspaper, the *Silver State*. When the first Silver Clubs were organized, he became state president. The announced purpose focused on one goal: revoking the 1873 suspension of silver coinage.
2. Thomas Wren had been one of the earliest settlers in Austin in 1864. A lawyer in mining litigation who had sharpened his skills in the California gold country, he settled in Eureka in the early 1870s. His reputation in both law and politics enabled him to be elected to the House of Representatives in 1876. He argued that the silver cause could be achieved without being tied to partisan politics.
3. Charles C. Wallace (often called "Black" or "Blackie" Wallace) had also arrived in Nevada in the 1860s, sampled the mining prospect in Austin and Hamilton, and finally located in Eureka. This became his home base for three decades, but he became a close associate of the executives of the Central Pacific and Southern Pacific railroads. He exercised his greatest influence in Carson City when the legislature was in session every two years.
4. George W. Cassidy, also of Eureka, was the fourth member of this silver quartet. He, too, had arrived in Nevada in the 1860s and participated in the "rush to White Pine." He had served in four sessions of the Nevada legislature (1873–79) and two terms as representative in Congress (1881–85). Cassidy was an odd political creature in that he was a successful Democrat during a time when the Republicans usually prevailed.

When the Silver League first came together, it tried to be nonpartisan, immune from the agendas of the two major parties. But to get a place on the ballot, it had to become a political party. When it did so in 1892, more than two-thirds of Nevada's voters cast their votes for the Silver slate. It was a lonely fledgling party in the larger political world, and its national affiliate, the Populist Party, lost decisively in the presidential election of that year. The Silver movement continued to hold first place in Nevada politics for about ten years, through the passionate election cycles of 1896 and 1900. William Jennings Bryan of Nebraska became the Democratic hero of miners, stockmen, and farmers throughout the West. The whirlwind died down with the arrival of a new century. In Nevada, discoveries of silver at Tonopah, gold in Goldfield, and copper in White Pine County shifted public attention to new issues and new possibilities.

Some Silver Party leaders soon found other roles. George Nixon, the Winnemucca banker, was the most successful. He moved to Goldfield after 1902 and became a mining baron in partnership with his Winnemucca friend George Wingfield. Nixon soon became a U.S. senator, chosen by legislators he had known during the Silver Party years. But by that time, the monetary controversy was a fading memory.

Victims of the White Man's Conquest: Native Americans in Retreat

The subculture that has been most frequently ignored by mainstream historians of Nevada is that of the Native Americans. The Humboldt corridor and the Central zone were the home territory to Shoshone and Northern Paiute bands for centuries before people of European descent began to trickle in, first as explorers with guns, then as emigrants with cattle that might be poached to feed hungry families, and finally as conquerors who swept the native peoples out of the way.

The tangled history of the relations between the Native peoples and the emigrant settlers has been retold many times. The last four decades of the nineteenth century produced a history of conquest and displacement that later generations have often deplored and tried to amend.

Joseph Walker's expedition was only the first episode of confrontation between the Native peoples and migrating pioneers.

Memories of this encounter faded rapidly; in fact it was virtually unknown among later white emigrants. But another, more serious showdown occurred twenty-seven years later with the so-called Pyramid Lake War.

In the spring of 1860, just as the rush to the Comstock Lode was beginning, two bloody battles occurred on the lower Truckee River between reckless bands of white men from the vicinity of Carson and Virginia City and a band of Paiutes. The Paiutes were wrongfully accused of a murder at a frontier station. In the first battle, the Paiutes, defending their home territory, killed about seventy-six attackers. In the second encounter, at least a hundred Native Americans lost their lives.

From the 1860s until the late 1870s, pioneer settlers had recurring nightmares about the "Indian threat." Newspapers and local folklore gave more attention to the confrontations than to the many instances of exploitation and cruelty inflicted on the Native Americans. In 1863, Territorial Governor James W. Nye, who was also the Indian Agent for the U.S. government, signed a treaty with the Shoshone chief known as Te-moak that was intended to respect traditional rights of Indians and stop the depredations against emigrants and settlers. The meaning and intention of this so-called Ruby Valley Treaty were still being debated 150 years later.

A carefully assembled book by Colonel Daniel C. B. Rathbun lists about thirty "battles" in Nevada between 1860 and 1869, mostly in the Humboldt region or nearby. All were brief skirmishes; none was nearly as serious as the 1860 encounters at Pyramid Lake. The small bands of Indians were widely scattered, foraging as their ancestors had done for centuries, and occasionally coming into conflict with white settlers.

The U.S. Army located camps or posts at several places across the Northeast during and soon after the Civil War. Four of the best known were Fort Ruby (1862–69), Dun Glen (1862–66), Fort McDermit (1865–89) and Fort Halleck (1867–86).

Many scholars have guessed at the number of Native Americans living in the Great Basin in the early years of statehood, but there is little reliable information prior to 1880. The U.S. census that year counted 62,266 residents of Nevada. Of this number, 2,803 were Indians, and about half of these lived in the North-Center.

SARAH WINNEMUCCA: THE PAIUTE PRINCESS

Sarah Winnemucca belatedly became the most famous woman who lived in northern Nevada in the nineteenth century. Her Paiute father had much influence among the Native American bands of the lower Humboldt. Born about 1844, probably in the Big Meadows, Sarah remembered and wrote about the violence between the conquering pioneers and her people. She gradually became a literate political activist, writing and lecturing with such passion that her reputation gained her a place as one of two Nevadans in Statuary Hall in the nation's capitol in Washington, D.C., a century after her death.

With the help of the famous Peabody sisters of Boston, Sarah Winnemucca published *Life Among the Paiutes: Their Wrongs and Claims* in 1883, the first autobiography by a Native American woman. But during her lifetime, she was often regarded with contempt by her Anglo contemporaries in Nevada and even by members of her own tribe.

Among the many episodes of Sarah's tragic life, eloquently described by Sally Zanjani, was her effort to provide education for children of her tribe. After her triumphant lecture tour in the East in 1883, she returned to Nevada, lived for a time on the Pyramid Lake Indian Reservation, and then returned to the Big Meadows to operate a school for Paiute children. The effort continued for about four years. Although she still had the help of Elizabeth Peabody of Boston and many testimonials for her work as a teacher, her health and the school failed, and she moved north to Montana, where she died several years later at the age of forty-seven under strange circumstances. Through her life of wandering, the Big Meadows was the setting for her fondest dreams.

The narrative that flows from *Life Among the Paiutes* is one segment of the epic of the defeat and decline of the Native American culture in the northern Great Basin. The early history of the region is speckled with episodes of hunger and suffering by displaced Indians and by fear and suspicion on the part of miners, ranchers, and other settlers.

During the twentieth century, the number of Native Americans who made their homes in the North-Center declined relative to the general population. In 2010, there were nine reservations and two colonies in the region. The total number of individuals who identified themselves as American Indians or Alaskan Natives in these seven counties comprised about five percent of the total.

THE FIRST DAWN OF WOMAN SUFFRAGE

The North-Center was an early testing ground for the idea of woman suffrage movement in the far West. While the first decisive moves to give women the right to vote came in Utah and Wyoming territories, Nevada was the first state to give serious consideration to the idea. The Humboldt basin produced some of the most vocal champions of this long-delayed reform.

The first woman to challenge the all-male regimen on Nevada's political frontier was Laura DeForce Gordon, who lectured about the necessity of equal rights for women in many assembly halls of California and Nevada in the late 1860s. She and her husband visited both Austin and Treasure City, where she promoted woman suffrage with evangelical passion. Her message resonated in many parts of the region. At the same time, a similar amendment to extend voting rights to African–Americans gained support.

In 1869, State Senator M. S. Bonnifield of Humboldt County led a coalition of legislators who proposed an amendment to remove the word "male" from the section of the Nevada Constitution that identified those citizens who were entitled to vote. The measure was approved in both the Senate and Assembly. In Nevada, a proposed constitutional amendment must be approved by two consecutive sessions of the legislature before it can be submitted to the voters for final approval. Bonnifield was a pillar of political influence in northern Nevada, as well as co-owner of the *Humboldt Register*. He did not hesitate to use its pages to support the idea of woman's franchise. The cause also had support from the *Elko Independent*.

In April and May 1870, the *Register* reported on plans for a convention of dignitaries from several western states and territories to meet in Winnemucca on July 4. They would organize a campaign to advance woman suffrage during the 1871 legislative session.

A small group of suffragist supporters met on that day, but in Battle Mountain rather than Winnemucca. Laura DeForce Gordon was present, along with several other feminist leaders from California. Senator Bonnifield chaired the meeting and a reporter from the *Elko Independent*, John I. Ginn, served as recording secretary. Gordon delivered one of the most rousing speeches.

> Taken as a whole the speech of Mrs. Gordon (given without notes) was one of those rare, intellectual efforts in which all parts of the discourse were so completely put together that it might seem to have been created by a single stroke. The hearty applause elicited by striking hits, beautifully rounded periods, and eloquent perorations, soon merged into the most intense enthusiasm; and as the most chaste, elegant and forcible words in the language poured from her lips, like a stream of liquid fire, her eyes sparkled with animation, her graceful form swayed to and fro, and her tapered fingers moved through air in unison with her burning words, the whole audience became electrified and listened with bated breath, as if in fear that a gem might fall unheeded.

This Elko writer's eloquent description of Gordon's performance may suggest an interest beyond the merely political. In any case, the meeting tried to organize a network of committees in each of Nevada's fourteen counties, but the cause found little support in the newspapers of Virginia and Carson City. When the proposed amendment came before the legislature the second time in 1871, it languished and died. Amendments to extend the franchise to women were introduced several times during the 1880s and 1890s, only to fail for lack of sufficient support. Finally, in the early years of the twentieth century, leaders emerged in Nevada who enabled the state to join the national suffrage movement.

Although reform movements affecting money, Native Americans, and women's rights failed in the nineteenth century, they formed a basis for changes in the twentieth.

CHAPTER SIX

Turn of the Century

Economics and Culture

A LABYRINTH OF IMPRESSIONS

The North-Center was a testing ground for the land-distribution policies offered by the federal government in the nineteenth century. Before Nevada became a state, Congress had already approved the Pacific Railway Act awarding the "checkerboard" land grant to the companies that built the railroad. This made the Central Pacific the largest property owner in the state, with more than 5 million acres.

Another law enacted by Congress during the Civil War, the Homestead Act of 1862, had a much smaller impact in Nevada. It offered 640 acres at bargain terms to a family that would cultivate the land. But in the water-scarce high desert, such a seemingly generous offer had little practical application.

An additional opportunity for settlers, at least in theory, came in a series of land grants. One law offered 3.9 million acres to be sold for the support of public education. It required that two specific sections (one square mile each) of every township (36 square miles) be sold to support schools.

These arrangements had usually served small farmers well in the rainy parts of the East and Middle West. It was a cruel failure in the Great Basin, where a generation of dedicated settlers "bit the dust" under the infrequent and stingy rain clouds. Moreover, the land surveys often placed a checkerboard square on a rock pile, a steep slope, or a dry lake. Most settlers failed after a year or two. Like the prospectors, they soon became exhausted and disappointed. Here, water supplies were almost as rare as precious metal discoveries.

The Ruby Mountains and the Snake Range beckoned another kind of pioneer, one who occasionally prospered where the small farmers failed. These were the men who owned large herds of cattle and sheep and could run their animals on unclaimed public acres. The Great Basin offered many advantages to this class of investors. Where the mountain peaks loom far above the adjacent valleys, the higher slopes catch the airborne Pacific moisture that has evaded the Cascades and the Sierra Nevada. Winter snow melts into the riparian canyons, nourishing the rich grasses that make northeastern Nevada excellent grazing terrain.

After the prospectors had made their first sweep across the upper Basin, and after the Central Pacific had stretched its ribbon of iron along the Humboldt, livestock owners drove large herds onto the high desert. Cowboys and sheep men could be hired for little pay.

While the federal policies enacted to help family farmers were disappointing failures in Nevada, as the acreage that could be acquired by homesteading or under the Desert Land Act was inadequate for traditional small-scale horticulture, the men who profited from the land grants were not the yeomen farmers that Congress intended. Instead, they were a few land barons who could identify water sources, file for rights under the doctrine of prior appropriation, wait for the small farmers to fail, and then move large herds among the valleys and water holes. Usually they did not have long to wait.

THE SPARKS–TINNAN–HARRELL DOMAIN

As early as the 1840s, wagon train emigrants on their way to California exploited the grasses of the northern Humboldt headwaters for feeding their tired cattle. They had called the region the Thousand Springs because of the scattered sources of water that appeared in the canyons and uplands early in the year. In the 1880s, two former Confederate soldiers from Texas rediscovered the region's possibilities for nourishing livestock on a long-term basis.

After the Civil War, John Sparks of Texas drove several herds of cattle from Texas to the Union Pacific railroad in Wyoming. By 1881, he had teamed up with another Texan, John Tinnan, to buy property in southern Idaho and in the adjacent Thousand Springs area in Nevada. In November 1883, the *Elko Independent* called Sparks and Tinnan "the cattle kings of the west" (Young and Sparks, 103). These monarchs of the high desert probably did not know how many animals they had on the range and certainly did not want the county assessors to know.

The two Texans shared a profitable operation for a few years until they encountered two obstacles. First, a long drought in 1886–89 dried up the forage. Next came a devastating winter in 1889–90, when blizzards killed more than half of their cattle and sheep on the range. In the shake out that followed these disasters, Sparks formed a new partnership with Andrew J. Harrell, another sagebrush baron, and they gradually recovered financially. He gave increasing attention to a showplace ranch in Washoe Valley, which he called the Alamo in honor of the Texas fort made famous in the Mexican War.

As Sparks shifted his focus westward to the Sierra foothills, he became more involved in Nevada's politics. In 1902, he was elected governor, defeating another eastern Nevada rancher, A.C. Cleveland of Spring Valley in White Pine County. Sparks was re-elected in 1906 but died in office less than two years later. During his last years, Sparks specialized in breeding and showing purebred animals.

THE ADAMS–McGILL EMPIRE

Jewett W. Adams, a Yankee from Vermont, is a good example of a man who prospered in politics and business while most other Nevadans struggled and went broke. Arriving in Nevada in 1864, he developed a profitable freighting business and became a member of the state militia. In 1874, he was elected lieutenant governor, which made him Adjutant General of Nevada State Militia. In those days, this was a high-profile position. During the next year, when rumors spread about possible Indian uprisings in Elko and White Pine counties, he made a well-publicized visit to that region. Later in the 1870s, when the "charcoal burners' war" occurred in Eureka, he was called to duty there. On these trips, he also saw much of the potential rangeland of central and eastern Nevada.

Adams was re-elected lieutenant governor in 1878, ran successfully for governor in 1882, but was defeated when he sought a second term four years later. During his time in public office, he carefully watched the registers in the State Land Office in Carson

City, where claims for land titles were recorded. When a claimant defaulted on his payments, Adams often bought the parcel at a bargain if it had a stream on the property or nearby. Thus, he accumulated many strategic sites over the years and became the largest taxpayer in White Pine County. In the mid-1880s, he moved 5,000 head of cattle onto the rangelands of White Pine and northern Lincoln and Nye counties.

In 1898, Jewett Adams formed a partnership with William McGill, another former Comstock resident who had shifted his interests eastward and brought thousands of animals onto the ranges. His home ranch was on the slopes of the Schell Creek range in White Pine County. Adams and McGill expanded their access to strategic streams and watering holes in northern Nye and Lincoln counties as well and formed a corporation in 1912. They eventually controlled 98,000 acres of ranch- and rangeland and produced thoroughbred cattle as well as thousands of sheep. For many years, they operated a meatpacking plant in Ely.

The Adams–McGill partnership prospered into the early years of the twentieth century. Adams retired to San Francisco in about 1915, leaving most of the management responsibilities to McGill. While the business made profits during World War I, it fell on hard times soon after. Adams died in 1920; his partner lived three more years. Their empire disintegrated in litigation.

THE LOWER HUMBOLDT IN 1905

The cattle and sheep barons did not control the entire North-Center. While they reigned in most of the eastern half of the region, a different scenario unfolded in parts of the lower Humboldt.

A Winnemucca newspaper owner, Allen C. Bragg, became editor of the *Silver State* in November 1904. To get acquainted with his newly acquired readers, he made an extended series of tours within Humboldt County, which at that time included 16,000 square miles (before Pershing County had been detached).

Bragg traveled more than 1,200 miles by horse carriage over five months and tried to visit every settlement, ranch, and mine in the vast county. The mosaic that emerged in his newspaper columns was finally assembled seventy years later, when volunteers in the North Central Nevada Historical Society based in Winnemucca did the necessary editorial work to assemble his writings.

Finding warm welcomes and examples of frontier persistence everywhere he went, he reported on healthy herds, pleasant farms, and orchards and gardens in abundance. The 1905 readers of Bragg's odyssey were invited to consider Humboldt County and other parts of Nevada as an Arcadian paradise poised to become an economic dynamo. His essays are typical of someone who arrived in a place with high hopes for prosperity, became enchanted by its strange beauty, and after a short time moved on to presumably greener pastures.

He was especially impressed by what he saw in the southern part of the county, which at that time included the Big Meadows. The community of Lovelock that had evolved over the years was neither a boomtown nor a rowdy railroader's haven. Its transition differed from most other Nevada towns, because it evolved slowly on an agricultural base.

Lovelock has received little attention from state historians because it did not have a newspaper before 1892 and then suspended publication two years later. From then until 1898, there was no locally printed journal to chronicle the town's business. Prospectors established several mining districts in the adjacent mountains, but none produced enough pay dirt to justify their efforts. Early settlers in the Big Meadows had neither mining bonanzas nor the vast grazing lands of the upper Humboldt to attract attention. But while the Desert Land Act of 1877 did not help families who struggled in most parts of Nevada, it did serve the settlers on the lower Humboldt better than most. At first, they usually raised wheat but over time shifted to alfalfa hay to feed their cattle and to sell elsewhere.

Those who selected these Meadows for their homes learned over the years that the flow of water from their little river was not dependable. The seasons of heavy runoff were usually excellent for their fields and local grazing, but dry seasons occurred too often. The drought of the late 80s had a severe impact in the Big Meadows, because most of the river's diminished flow was diverted upstream.

John Townley, the most thorough chronicler of nineteenth-century Nevada agricultural history, offered a summary: "During the 1890s, Lovelock was the 'Cinderella' of western Nevada agriculture. Its excellent soil and climate produced bumper crops of grain and forage for a growing population."

During the 1890s, Nevadans passed through a period of despair. Virtually all of the rich mines of the bonanza era were dormant. In 1900, only $2.6 million of metal and mineral production was recorded; in 1875, it had had reported $35 million. As the nineteenth century drew to an end, a few prospectors were still flitting through the mountains like grasshoppers in the sagebrush. Only a handful struck pay dirt.

Small farmers were homesteading or squatting on their parcels like jackrabbits and squirrels. Overhead, the livestock barons were circling like eagles and hawks. Even so, the livestock businesses had also been through a painful decade; and while the number of cattle and sheep on the range had increased since the devastating drought and the freezing winter of 1889–90, things still did not seem right to those who had weathered the storms.

Population figures help us recognize the sparse human presence in the North-Center at the beginning of the twentieth century. The 1900 census counted only 42,335 residents in Nevada, down from 62,266 in 1880 (which had been considered a lean year compared with the bonanza period of the mid-1870s). Some commentators on the Atlantic fringe questioned whether Nevada had enough citizens to maintain its place as a state in the Federal Union.

These critics had a few facts to support their argument. The most populous county, Washoe (including Reno) had 9,141 residents. Storey County, the home of the famous Comstock Lode, had withered to the point where it had only 8,806. In the North-Center, the official census provided the numbers shown in table 6.1.

Nevada had several peculiarities that distinguished it from other states. It was not only the most thinly populated, but it also had a highly transient, ethnically mixed population. Of its total residents, about a fourth were foreign born, and another fourth had parents who had come from foreign countries. Men outnumbered women by a ratio of about six to four.

At the end of the nineteenth century, Nevada was a state whose primary political mission was to revive mining by boosting the price of silver. It had no other reliable economic base.

TABLE 6.1. U.S. CENSUS FIGURES, 1900.

COUNTIES	TOTAL COUNTY POPULATION	PRINCIPAL TOWNS
Churchill	830	New River 276
Elko	5,688	Elko 849
Eureka	1,954	Eureka 785
Humboldt	4,463	Lovelock* 1,204; Winnemucca 1,110
Lander	1,534	Austin (2 precincts) 702; Battle Mountain 365
Lincoln	3,825**	Pioche 282; Delamar 904; Panaca 339; Las Vegas 30
Nye	1,140	Belmont 242
White Pine	1,961	Ely 525
Total	Approx. 20,000	

* Lovelock was the largest town in the region according to the 1900 census. Two decades later, Humboldt County was divided to give Lovelock its own separate county, Pershing.
** In 1900, Lincoln County still included all the area that later became Clark County. It was divided in 1909 to allow Las Vegas, the recently established railroad town, to become a county seat.

Nearly all its mines were inactive; its livestock business was still worried about the possibility of another devastating winter or a prolonged drought. Ranchers had learned not to rely entirely on the rangelands but to raise and bale hay for winter use. And prospectors had almost abandoned hope of the next bonanza.

In the election of 1900, about 10,000 voters went to the polls in Nevada's fourteen counties, about a third of them in the North-Center. The outcome was disappointing because the populist candidate for President, Silver–Democrat William Jennings Bryan, won easily in Nevada, but he lost overwhelmingly for a second time to Republican William McKinley, and the detested goldbugs of Wall Street. Nevada's political leadership still consisted of Senators William M. Stewart and John P. Jones, the two old senators who had been repeatedly elected by successive sessions of the state legislature since the days of the Comstock bonanza. Nevada's cultural life reflected its general economic despair.

But after 1900, Nevada's stunted economy gradually began reviving, as fresh cultural, social, and economic breezes blew across the North-Center from unexpected directions.

CHAPTER SEVEN

Government Experiments in Churchill County

The Newlands Project

In 1861, when the first session of the Territorial Legislature identified nine counties and drew lines on its crude map, Churchill County was one of the most problematic. It was only a wide swath of alkali, sand, and rugged mountains with very few residents. Forty years later, that was still the situation. Because of its thinly scattered population, Churchill was the last Nevada county in the nineteenth century to be organized and to have a functioning county seat.

After three unsuccessful attempts, a local government center finally appeared in 1868 at Stillwater, which had once been a station on the Overland Stage line. Its population at that time was reported to be about 150, approximately one-third of the number living in the entire county. In 1900, Churchill still had only 830 residents, most of them families or hired men tending cattle that grazed in the region where the Carson River gradually becomes an alkaline sink. The county lacked the advantages of a railroad; herders who wanted to get their cattle and sheep to market usually drove them 30 miles west to Wadsworth on the Truckee River. No productive mines had ever been established in this skeleton of a county.

But the new century soon brought a promising new opportunity. The region between Carson Lake and the Carson Sink had come to the attention of Francis G. Newlands, Nevada's sole congressional representative. He belonged to a younger generation of politicians with more progressive values; during his ten years in the House of Representatives (1893–1903), Newlands advanced the idea of "reclaiming" the deserts of the far West through careful water management.

After several unsuccessful attempts to get help from the national level, he shared a big prize, the National Reclamation Act of 1902, signed by President Theodore Roosevelt. This law enabled the federal government to lend money acquired from the sale of public lands to western regions for irrigation and cultivation.

One of the first experiments began in the center of Churchill County. The planners of the Newlands project anticipated that as many as 400,000 acres could be plowed, irrigated and made productive. The federal government financed diversions of part of the Truckee River—whose natural course course is northward to Pyramid Lake—into the watershed of the Carson River basin. The project authorized Derby Dam on the Truckee River and a 31-mile canal to transfer half its flow into the Carson basin.

While the dam and canal were under construction, the town of Fallon developed at a faster pace than its nearest northern neighbor, Lovelock, more than 50 miles distant. It was laid out in an orderly, rectangular pattern on farmland previously owned by Mike Fallon, a rancher who had also operated a post office for several years. The town was planned with the encouragement of the newly created U.S. Reclamation Service (USRS) in plots of 80 or 160 acres. A few fraudulent promoters tried to defraud naive settlers but usually with little success.

The Newlands agricultural experiment encountered many unforeseen challenges. When the first water flowed down the canal in 1906, about 108 ranches were waiting, but over the next few years the Carson River and Truckee canal provided fewer acre-feet than promised. Given the sandy and alkali-laden soil, it was often necessary to plow humus or manure into the ground for two or three years to provide an adequate organic base for crops. But the farmers who could produce alfalfa hay found ready markets, because the Southern Pacific built a railroad spur to Fallon in 1907.

Usually, farmers worried that they would not have enough water for irrigation, but in 1907, Fallon had to deal with one of the worst floods in the history of the region. Most settlers persisted, and by 1910 Fallon had a population of 1,625. Only a few towns in Nevada were larger.

Because of the erratic nature of the water supply, the Reclamation Service decided in 1911 to build a large reservoir west of

Fallon where the Truckee Canal joins the Carson River. Construction of the Lahontan Dam between 1911 and 1914 employed about 800 workers, and while it disrupted agricultural production for a while, it provided greater long-term assurance of a reliable water supply for the hay and crops. The dam was designed to hold nearly 300,000 acre-feet and to generate electrical power. Its facilities were in service by the time World War I broke out. The improvements allowed the Newlands Project to expand production of crops and animals.

Both the U.S. Reclamation Service and the Lahontan Valley ranchers had much to learn during the first twenty years of the Project's operations. While the initial plan assumed that the diverted waters of the Carson and Truckee Rivers could irrigate more than 400,000 acres of land, this estimate had to be revised sharply downward, first to 206,000 acres in 1916 and then to 87,500 acres ten years later—less than one-fourth of its original intended size. Even then, irrigation water finally allotted was not assured. Lawsuits initiated by upstream users continued for decades.

In 1913, when the Lahontan Dam project was nearing completion, the U.S. government filed a so-called friendly lawsuit to identify and clarify existing water rights on the Truckee River and to learn how much unappropriated flow might be claimed legally for diversion to the new reservoir. This litigation proved to be not so friendly, because it involved property owners at Lake Tahoe, an upstream electrical power company, farmers, other users in the Reno–Sparks area, and many others who had claims. The case—*U.S. v. Orr Ditch*—was under adjudication in federal courts for thirty-one years. In 1944, a judge finally announced a settlement, with nearly all parties agreeing to a consent decree. In the end, most Lahontan farmers felt the decree gave them less water than they had been promised.

In spite of frequent disappointments, Fallon farmers experimented with many crops beyond alfalfa. In the earliest years, the Reclamation Service and local investors encouraged the production of sugar beets. A large processing plant was constructed and many planters took up the challenge, but within a few years the venture failed because leafhoppers followed the farmers into the fields and decimated their crops.

During the 1920s, cantaloupes became the crop of choice for a large number of farmers. The Heart of Gold melons were widely cultivated and widely advertised; for many years, it was reasonably successful. Some farmers also raised potatoes, onions, celery, and asparagus. Dairy and poultry operations all attracted producers.

In 1926, a time of prosperity, the U.S. Reclamation Service transferred responsibility for managing the Project to a newly created local authority—the Truckee-Carson Irrigation District (TCID). It seemed to be a logical transition, but soon new challenges arose. The years 1928–32 were a period of prolonged drought, when little snow fell in the Sierra and little water flowed down to Lahontan.

Then came the Great Depression of the 1930s, when prices of all agricultural products plummeted. Residents of Churchill County, like most Americans, looked to the federal government for relief. The New Deal brought more and different federal agencies into the economic life of the region. The Civilian Conservation Corps (CCC), with its teams of young men, helped improve the irrigation systems and was especially appreciated. When the drought abated in the middle 1930s, and the Depression seemed to be losing its grip, Fallon resumed its slow growth. By the end of the decade, the little city had resumed the pastoral, orderly pattern of its earlier years. In 1940, Fallon and its vicinity had a population of 4,646.

The Naval Air Station Since 1941

World War II affected Fallon more thoroughly than any community in the North-Center. In the early 1940s, local businessmen, with the support of Senator Pat McCarran, encouraged the U.S. Army Corps of Engineers to develop an airstrip south of Fallon as a training station for pilots. The military planners of that era were searching the inland West for places where they might train young aviators for combat. Churchill County was immediately affected.

Fallon residents welcomed the chance to serve the nation in a time of war. For more than three intense years, commercial activity surged and local businesses prospered. The Navy soon took over from the Army and enlarged the airfield to train more aviators and aircrews. Naval Auxiliary Air Station Fallon was commissioned in

June 1944, and the town awaited arrival of a thousand cadets to add to construction personnel already on the job.

Within Fallon, an acute housing problem developed as construction workers and military personnel arrived, some with families. The newspapers printed frequent reports of rent gouging. Local schools, the water supply network, sewer, and hospital systems soon felt the impact. The wartime shortage of building materials compounded the problems.

The mobilization frenzy peaked during the last year of World War II. Soon after the war ended in 1945, the Navy began to dismantle or abandon its hardware more quickly than it had been built. In June 1946, the Station was placed on "caretaker" status with the county government responsible for administration. Some facilities were offered to Native American communities.

Less than five years later, however, when the Korean War began, the Navy reopened its dormant station and built longer runways to accommodate the new jet-propelled planes, absorbing several ranches in the process. By the time that conflict ended, the Navy had become a growing—and permanent—neighbor. Later, in 1972, when the Vietnam conflict was underway, the Navy redesignated it as Naval Air Station Fallon (NAS), dropping the restrictive label "auxiliary" from its name.

By 1996, NAS Fallon, nicknamed TOPGUN, was a major base in the United States for training Navy pilots. It had taken control of 84,000 acres of surrounding land for use as bombing and electronic warfare ranges. It was also a crucial unit in the nation's early warning system against a possible enemy attack.

The Fallon farmers of the 1940s could not have anticipated the long-term effects of welcoming the military establishment as a close neighbor. Canyons and fields previously used for grazing were needed for other purposes. When Navy authorities looked for land suitable for expanded runways or target practice, they occasionally met protests from livestock owners who had used the ranges in a different way. Several large areas of mostly barren desert were set aside for bombing and gunnery practice and designated as "restricted areas." Occasionally a motorist on U.S. Highway 50 would hear the roar of jet planes overhead and see the puffs of dust in the distance. But Fallon residents were a continually reminded that they had been inducted into a more complicated world.

Water Challenges Since 1944

The *Orr Ditch* settlement of 1944 did not bring the matter of Truckee-Carson Irrigation District water litigation to a close, as Fallon expected. In 1973, the conflict reappeared in another form, when lawyers for the U.S government and the Pyramid Lake Indian Reservation reopened the case to seek more rights for the Indians. These claims involved property owners at Lake Tahoe, the growing cities of Reno and Sparks, and the Indian Reservation, as well as TCID—all of whom had been promised rights to the Truckee River by the *Orr Ditch* decree. In this case, the U.S. government was an adversary, not a friend, of the Fallon water users. The case finally went to the U.S. Supreme Court, where it ended in 1983. To the relief of Fallon residents, the 1944 decree was reaffirmed.

Other challengers of TCID were upstream on the Carson River watershed, in the fields of Carson Valley where Nevada's first settlement was built in 1851. And just below were the mills of the famous Comstock Lode that had refined multimillions of gold and silver in the 1860s and 1870s. Reconciling their prior claims with those of the Fallon users was another ongoing problem.

Court judgments did not resolve all the objections; weather and the fickle nature of the flow from the rivers continued to haunt the Newlands Project. In 2008, almost exactly a century after its origin, a flood breached the banks of the Truckee Canal and damaged many homes and other property in Fernley. Users dependent on Lahontan Reservoir had to cope with reduced flow for many months in addition to the expense of rebuilding.

Stillwater, the Wetlands, and Native Americans

At least two other dimensions of federal government activity added to the diversity of Churchill County—Indian colonies and wildlife refuges.

The tiny hamlet of Stillwater, 12 miles east of Fallon, did not receive much attention as the seat of Churchill County (1868–1903) and even less after it lost that dubious distinction. It had fewer than 500 residents through most of the twentieth century, mostly Native Americans attached to their ancestral land near the marshes and sinks at the lowest point on the Carson River. The Bureau of Indian Affairs serves the Fallon Paiute-Shoshone Reservation and the smaller Fallon Paiute-Shoshone Colony. A local author and scholar, Margaret Wheat, made Native American handicrafts the focus of her studies, and through publications brought their artistry to the attention of the wider public.

One resource that attracted Native Americans to this area in prehistoric times was the abundance of plants and waterfowl in the wetlands. These were threatened as more water was diverted upstream for agriculture and as the Navy conducted its noisy exercises. In recent years, a network of sloughs and ditches east and south of Fallon has become a favorite pilgrimage site for professional ornithologists and amateur birdwatchers. But the recurrent question was how all these interests—agricultural, military, Native American, and wildlife—could be reconciled.

In 1949, the federal government established part of the area as a wildlife sanctuary. Over the next half-century, the U.S Fish and Wildlife Service managed to expand the protected area and to acquire additional water rights. By 2011, farmers, naturalists, and duck hunters were encouraged by developments, but it turned out to be an unusually abundant water year in the Newlands system.

Project Shoal

The Bureau of Reclamation and U.S. Navy, by the 1960s, considered the valley of the Carson Sink a vast laboratory for experimental agricultural and military uses. Early in that decade, yet another federal agency applied another kind of testing to this terrain. This one, we now know in retrospect, was much more dangerous and potentially more deadly for Churchill County, for it involved the testing of a nuclear device.

Prior to 1963, the United States Atomic Energy Commission (AEC) had conducted hundreds of atomic explosions above ground at the Nevada Test Site (NTS) northwest of Las Vegas. The mushroom clouds became symbols of the nation's Cold War effort to stay ahead of the Soviet Union in weaponry. Ironically, it became clear that many illnesses and deaths among "downwinders" could be attributed to the radioactive fallout from these tests. In 1963, the U.S. and Soviet governments signed a limited test-ban treaty agreeing to stop detonating bombs above ground.

Immediately after the treaty was signed, the Atomic Energy Commission (AEC) was ready with an alternative—an underground test of a 12-kiloton device at Sand Springs only 30 miles southeast of Fallon. Residents had been prepared well in advance for the event; the roar of the explosion and cloud of dust were expected. As author Michon Mackedon wrote in her book *Bombast*, "For a year leading up to 26 October, the community of Fallon was bathed in the promises of health and wealth. Consistent with the old promotional approach, the potential for accidental fallout was barely addressed. Consistent with the new promotional approach, the AEC waved a wand with dollar signs over the community."

Responsibility for monitoring the post-blast site and protecting people who can now wander the area later passed to the Department of Energy and then to the Department of Defense. But in an era of budget cutting, Fallon residents have wondered if the U.S. government will remember its watchdog responsibilities at the site. Fortunately for the health of subsequent residents of Churchill County, the results of Project Shoal did not encourage the government to conduct more experiments.

LOCAL GOVERNMENT AND CULTURAL INSTITUTIONS

The Courthouse

The only wooden courthouse in Nevada is located at the hub of historical Fallon. Built in 1903 soon after the Newlands Project was authorized, it was the most classical building in town, with Ionic columns rising to complement a two-story portico. Its front faced Maine Street and the south portion of the Carson Basin, soon to be under cultivation. In the 1940s, with local government business expanding, the county considered replacing it with a more modern structure but decided instead to construct an annex on the north side. So Fallon responded to its growth without destroying its traditional turn-of-the-century monument to local government.

The Library

Churchill County residents began a lending library as early as 1918, thanks to a few volunteers who collected donated books. County commissioners added nominal financial support in 1925. The collection of printed materials had several temporary homes before 1966, when the Max C. Fleischmann Foundation made a major gift, stimulating support from the federal and state governments and local contributors. The new facility opened in 1967, and, although it eventually became somewhat cramped, it was still actively serving patrons more than four decades later.

The College

When the Board of Regents of the University of Nevada embraced the concept of community colleges in the early 1970s, Fallon was one of the first towns to request its services. The Churchill County school board provided the initial framework for an experiment, and Western Nevada Community College (WNCC), based in Carson City, became the conduit for state support. The Fallon Center occupied its first building in 1981. The fledgling institution, bolstered by attending personnel from the Naval Air Station, held its first commencement in 1996 and was serving more than 1,200 students in attractive classrooms by 1998. Subsequent electronic improvements attracted many more clients who otherwise would not have considered higher education.

The recession of 2008–10 brought sharp downward adjustments. The number of instructors was reduced, along with classroom opportunities offered to students.

The Museum and Oats Park Art Center

During the final decades of the twentieth century, Churchill County developed an excellent small museum to display items that offer visual examples of the region's diverse natural and recorded history. The geographical setting, the life and culture of prehistoric peoples, and the development of the Newlands Project and Naval Air Station are all illustrated for the casual viewer. The museum has also published an annual volume of studies and reflections on the region's past. Few museums in the state can match it for professional excellence in representing local culture.

Another tangible example of Churchill County's growing appreciation of the community's possibilities is the Oats Park Arts Center, situated in a century-old school building that was constructed in 1914 and abandoned in 1954 after earthquake damage. After standing empty for three decades, the building was resurrected by a group of local citizens. The Churchill Arts Council rallied many community members who remembered their school days with affection. Building on that base, the Council raised about $10 million to adapt the structure to house a 350-seat auditorium, concert hall, three art galleries, plus a large kitchen and dining facilities.

Sarah Winnemucca statue at the California Trail Interpretive Center, near Elko. Courtesy of Jane Dixon.

Francis and Jane Lee, the first settlers to make a home in Panaca, 1864. Courtesy of Betty Hulse.

Sherman Station, home of the Elko Chamber of Commerce. Courtesy of Jane Dixon.

Oats Park Art Center, Fallon. Courtesy of Kirk Robertson.

Pioneer Hotel, home of the Western Folklife Center, Elko. Courtesy of Western Folklife Museum.

Washburn Ranch Cattle Drive near Winnemucca. Courtesy of Jack Hursh.

Northern Nevada Railway Museum, Ely. Courtesy of Betty Hulse.

Caliente Railroad Depot. Courtesy of Betty Hulse.

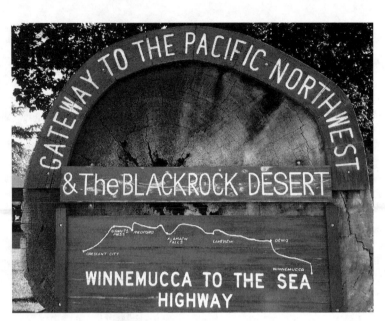

"Winnemucca to the Sea" promotion. Courtesy of Betty Hulse.

Headframe, Deep Ruth Shaft, near Ely. Photo by Larry Garside, courtesy of Nevada Bureau of Mines and Geology.

Barrick Goldstrike mine along the Carlin Trend. Courtesy of Barrick
Gold Company.

Snake Range, White Pine County. Photo by Kris Pizarro, courtesy of Nevada Bureau of Mines and Geology.

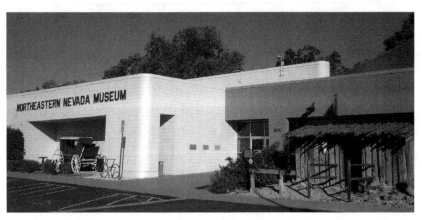

Northeastern Nevada Museum, Elko. Courtesy of Betty Hulse.

Wells, 7th St. 2008 earthquake. Photo by Nike Stake, courtesy of Nevada Bureau of Mines and Geology.

Lander County Courthouse, Battle Mountain. Courtesy of Betty Hulse.

California Trail Interpretive Center near Elko. Courtesy of Betty Hulse.

Humboldt County Museum, Winnemucca. Courtesy of Betty Hulse.

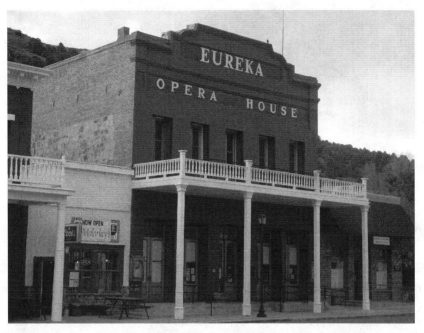

Eureka Opera House. Courtesy of Betty Hulse.

Great Basin National Park: Stella Lake and Wheeler Peak. Photo by
Jack Hursh, courtesy of Nevada Bureau of Mines and Geology.

Stokes Castle, Austin. Photo by Kris Pizarro, courtesy of Nevada Bureau of Mines and Geology.

Charcoal ovens, near Ely. Photo by Roy Cazier, courtesy of Nevada Bureau of Mines and Geology.

CHAPTER EIGHT

Copper Is King

New Technology in White Pine County

As the twentieth century opened, Nevada's mining economy had been stagnant for twenty years. The new discoveries at Tonopah in 1900 and Goldfield in 1902 seemed to validate the ever-present hopes of prospectors who had searched everywhere for the next bonanza. Yet both districts began to falter within a decade of opening. The bonanza of the next generation was not in silver or gold, but in copper.

The collapse of the boom at Hamilton and Treasure City in the 1870s brought a long pause in the metals industry in the central Great Basin. For a short time, the towns of Osceola in the Snake Range and Ward and Taylor south of Ely seemed to be potential replacements, but they never thrived. Cherry Creek to the north also held out promise for several years, but it too brought only false hopes and disappointment, even to its most dedicated residents. Such was the familiar pattern.

ELY, McGILL, RUTH

While silver and gold never lost their luster for the persistent prospectors, soon after 1900 a new generation of mining companies emerged, looking not for the "yellow metal" or the "white metal" but for the "red metal."

Copper deposits did not occur in easily identified veins or clusters like the precious metals of Virginia City. It occurred in a low-grade ore that had to be gouged in large quantities from open pits. Prospectors had recognized signs of this metal in the Egan Mountains 35 miles east of Hamilton as early as the 1870s. They formed the Robinson District, but no large investments were available until a quarter-century later. Both the absence of capital and lack of adequate transportation were obstacles until after 1900, when two prospectors identified a substantial deposit and caught the attention of a potential investor.

Within a few months, boosters of White Pine County proclaimed, "copper is king!" For a half-century, they had a credible point. Mining and smelting copper ore made this county the showplace of Nevada's metal-producing industry, well after the bonanzas at Tonopah and Goldfield had withered.

In 1902, Mark Requa, owner of the Eureka and Palisade Railroad (E&P), a branch line of the Central Pacific (mentioned in chapter 4), became interested in the Robinson district and purchased much of the known copper ore body. He considered extending his struggling E&P eastward about 75 miles from its terminal in Eureka to the new mines and the nearby town named Ruth, but that would have required grading and laying track across four intervening mountain ranges. It soon became obvious that a more feasible route for a connection with the transcontinental railroad would be to build a shorter link from the mines to Ely. From there, another line would extend north through the Steptoe Valley to connect with the Southern Pacific at a place called Cobre (the Spanish word for copper) east of Wells—140 miles distant. The terrain here was much easier, because it was through north-south valleys.

By 1905, Requa had arranged the necessary surveys and recruited allies among local businessmen and landowners. The Northern Nevada Railway became a legal entity on June 1; construction proceeded for the next year. Ely celebrated "Railroad Days" in September 1906, when the Cobre line arrived. During the same period, Requa organized the Nevada Consolidated Copper Co. Ely emerged as a viable commercial center at about the same time as the arrival of the first automobiles and electricity. It was not merely a "camp" in the miners' vocabulary but a commercial center with some of the amenities of the twentieth century.

Requa soon attracted the attention of the wealthy Guggenheim family of Philadelphia with its vast empire of ore processing and smelting ventures. As large fish swallow small fish, so the Guggenheims absorbed the young White Pine companies into their system. The largest of the Ely (Robinson) District mines and the Nevada Northern became a part of an international business venture to an extent previously unknown in Nevada. Requa was no longer needed at the end of 1906 and was dismissed, retired along with the horse and buggy in the cultural shift, but local residents honored his memory for several decades.

The once-sleepy town of Ely now hummed with commercial activity. Promotion and sale of lots brought speculators from distant places, including Tex Rickard, who had made a reputation for national promotion of Goldfield with well-publicized boxing matches.

Two or three years were necessary to arrange locations for the various components that served the new industry. Ruth, Kimberly, and Veteran, seven or eight miles west of Ely, grew up around the expanding mines where the ore was extracted. Eastward, on the other side, the ranchlands of William McGill on the slopes of the Schell Creek Range had access to a generous supply of water necessary for a mill and smelter, transferrable through a large pipeline. Though it was costly to refine and smelt low-grade ore in such a remote spot in the Basin, the essential components of water and space were available, and fuel could be imported by rail.

By the time Ely celebrated the completion of the Nevada Northern railroad in 1906, the new satellites were on the maps. The workers of Ruth blasted ore from underground mines or ever-expanding pits and loaded it into railroad cars. Trains of the Nevada Northern then hauled it through Ely on their way to the furnaces of McGill for refining. By 1907, copper ingots from McGill were on their way by rail to the Eastern markets. A twentieth-century version of the industrial revolution had sprouted in eastern Nevada.

A Multifaceted Nevada Subculture

Most of Ely's newly established neighbors were company towns, owned and managed by Nevada Consolidated under strict rules designed to provide a reliable and healthy work force. Miners and mill workers were typically an itinerant and unreliable flock, inclined to unpredictable moves from one camp to another. In this instance, the primary company offered them housing, markets, medical services, and recreation facilities at a modest cost. It was a benign form of community socialism sponsored by a capitalistic employer. Ruth, McGill, Kimberly, and Veteran (while it lasted) were all established on this basis.

Russell R. Elliott, a native son of McGill who for three decades was the most respected historian of Nevada, described the system in affectionate detail in his final book, *Growing Up in a Company Town*. Private businesses could operate only with the permission of the company on land available for leasing. Houses were assigned to managers and workers in distinct neighborhoods. In most communities, which consisted of large numbers of immigrants, different ethnic groups tended to cluster in their own sections. By this process, in the decade between 1910 and 1920, the new era of *copper* mining and new styles of communities were introduced in the so-called *silver* state.

Nevada Consolidated was not the only producer in the Robinson district, but it was by far the largest. A rival company with adjacent property was the Consolidated Copper Company. These two companies engaged in lawsuits over property lines and smelting arrangements for several years.

The copper mining business fluctuated with the economic health of the nation. During World War I, when copper was in great demand, Ely and its neighbors prospered. During the recession of the early 1920s, copper production in White Pine County was curtailed. It revived in the last half of the Roaring Twenties, only to crash again with the onset of the Great Depression in the early 1930s. In the worst years, Nevada Consolidated operated at only about fifteen percent of capacity. Yet over the long run, the Ely/Robinson district was the most profitable mining region in the state and one of the leading copper producers in the West during the early twentieth century.

During the early years of the Great Depression, Nevada Consolidated, which had been the state's leading producer of metals for two decades, was absorbed into the giant Kennecott Copper Corporation.

The Ely–Ruth–McGill triad functioned in this economic environment for an additional quarter-century, prospering during World War II and the Korean conflict. In 1958, Kennecott finally absorbed its long-term rival, Consolidated Copper, but in the interim the domestic copper industry became less competitive in the world market. The larger and deeper pits in the Robinson district made production of the low-grade ore more expensive, and production from newly developed foreign copper sites gradually undercut the domestic industry.

In the postwar era, the local labor union—like their fellow workers across America—demanded better pay and more benefits. Ten strikes occurred in White Pine between 1950 and 1980—two of them lasting several weeks. Meanwhile, Kennecott was gradually reducing its work force. The company announced in 1956 that it would sell off the houses and other property in Ruth and McGill, altering the long-term relationship that workers had relied on.

Another change came in 1976 when the six-year-old Environmental Protection Agency ruled that the smelter at McGill did not meet standards of new regulations for air quality. Kennecott and its local allies fought this finding in the political arena but merely delayed the inevitable. By 1983, copper production had dropped to the lowest level since 1935— the darkest period of the Great Depression. While the rest of the nation and the economy of Nevada were thriving, Ely and its neighbors were in recession.

In the first seventy years that the White Pine copper mines were active (1908–78), they yielded ore valued at twice the amount recorded on the Comstock Lode (in 2007 dollars). Geologists estimated that about 50 million additional tons of potential ore remained in the ground or in the mine dumps, but the low price of copper made further development unprofitable for many years.

After the end of Kennecott's long reign in 1983, Ely did not immediately collapse, as most mining-based regions had done in earlier times. The industrial, commercial, and residential structures of Ruth and McGill soon showed signs of the kind of decay that other boomtowns had known. But Ely had other resources on which it could draw; White Pine County had natural attractions that forestalled the usual fate of older camp siblings.

The county lost one-fourth of its residents between 1975 and 1985. The next twenty-five years saw a gentle fluctuation. In 1980, the population of White Pine was 8,167; 9,264 in 1990; 9,181 in 2000; and 10,030 in 2010. Economic help came in several forms: local initiatives, state government investment, and federal recognition. The Ely region was able to diversify, as no earlier mining community had been able to do.

Resumption of Mining

While White Pine's economy survived for several reasons, only one of them was mining. Prices of raw metals fluctuated, but newly financed ventures such as Magma Copper, Broken Hills, and Quadra Mining Ltd. processed large amounts of tailings and dug deeper into the pits, extracting rock that was considered too low-grade in the 1980s. These corporations were the modern prospectors, working not with pick and shovel but with high-tech equipment and in relation to the world-market prices of copper, gold, silver, and molybdenum.

No steady pattern is evident in this process. There were several peaks and valleys in investment and employment. In 2008, about 550 people were working in the pits and hills near where the towns of Ruth and Kimberly had once been. But this labor force was only about one fourth of the number that had been employed during the latter years of Kennecott's production.

Cultural Initiatives

In Ely, as with most other county seats, the courthouse holds a place of tradition and honor. It is situated a short distance east of the traditional commercial center, separated from the main street by an attractive small park. The current building dates from the earliest years of the copper boom. Built in 1908–09, it reflects what Ronald James, former director of Nevada's office of historical preservation, called "an eclectic style of architecture—combining Neo-classical and Italianate elements," crowned by a copper dome.

Ely's business community, often sensitive to its history, devised a way to celebrate the region's early ethnic diversity. In the late 1990s, the community created a "Renaissance Village" in the central part of the city, an assortment of buildings, artifacts, and outdoor art to celebrate its role as an American "melting pot" for immigrants. It included murals depicting the lives of various ethnic groups that had once formed the local human mix: Shoshones, Greeks, Serbs, Italians, Basques, Japanese, and Chinese, among

others, early in the century. When many of the city's original buildings decayed and were removed after Kennecott's departure, local
artists used the opened commercial spaces and walls for visual
offerings honoring local pioneers.

White Pine County Public Museum

White Pine County Public Museum was established in 1960 on
the initiative of Ely's business and professional women. In addition to local support, it received financial stimulation in the early
years from the Max C. Fleischmann Foundation of Reno. It holds
not only the traditional artifacts but also some of the equipment
donated by mining companies when they ceased active operations. A branch museum operates in McGill.

Railroad Restoration

During this process of reviving the city, the Northern Nevada Railway, which ceased operations in 1983, gradually rose from the
dead. Kennecott donated its Ely depot, other buildings, locomotives, and rolling stock to the White Pine Historical Foundation.
Local entities later began operating the Ghost Train of Old Ely
along a few miles of the original track as a tourist attraction.

Largely through such efforts, the old Nevada Northern depot
and other facilities in East Ely were gradually renovated. The
Nevada legislature joined the movement with an appropriation
in 1985, and the Nevada Department of Museums and History
furnished additional support. In 2006, the U.S. Park Service recognized it as a National Historic Landmark, and by 2015 it had
acquired more than a hundred pieces of antique rolling stock
and was a significant tourist attraction. It offers scheduled rides
that include the Ghost Train in October and the Polar Express at
Christmas.

Great Basin National Park

In 1987, White Pine County got a boost in tourism when Great
Basin National Park was born. This 78,600-acre region of rustic
alpine scenery became part of the national park system after a
sixty-year struggle between conservationists and local private
interests.

The park, about 60 miles southeast of Ely, is a remarkable example of the natural diversity of the Nevada landscape. From the valley foothills on the east and west sides (at about 6,000 feet above sea level), the Snake Range rises sharply. Several mountain peaks soar above 11,000 feet.

The highest—Wheeler Peak, at 13,063 feet—is usually crowned with snow much of the year. It has commanded the attention of Anglo–European explorers for nearly 200 years. Peter Skene Ogden, the Canadian fur trapper probably saw it in 1826; the waters that flow from adjacent canyons may have saved his life. Many other explorers, including Egan and Simpson and their crews, passed through Sacramento Pass, a relatively low saddle in the Snake Range.

By the early 1870s, settlers and prospectors were beginning to occupy the alluvial fans of the Snake Range. One of the earliest men to take up land and bring a family to the eastern slopes was Absalom Lehman, who claimed several hundred acres along a rushing stream. About a decade later, he discovered and explored the remarkable caverns nearby. The subterranean caves gradually yielded their mysteries and beauties to the eyes of amateur spelunkers. Reports of hundreds of stalactites and stalagmites within dozens of colorful chambers eventually caught the attention of officials in Carson City.

The first Nevada politician to emphasize the potential public value of the caves was State Engineer James G. Scrugham. He became the leading advocate in the movement to have the site declared a national monument in 1922. He also proposed that the entire region, including the high peaks of the Snake Range, be identified as a national park.

Another six decades elapsed before his proposal became a reality. Whenever conservationists and naturalists promoted the idea of a federally managed area to preserve the natural beauty of the Snake Range for future generations, they ran into determined opposition from local livestock owners and mining men who objected to the limitations that a national park would impose. Finally, in 1986, Congress arranged the necessary compromises, and President Ronald Reagan signed the bill into law. Since then, Great Basin National Park has been one of the treasures in the far Western panorama of scenic natural resources.

Darwin Lambert, a sensitive observer, offers the best concise history of the Park.

Low in the Snake Valley [on the east side] there is little plant growth except scattered greasewood shrubs. When you move up the gradual slope, you soon find shadscale, followed by sagebrush, rabbitbrush, and other shrubs. In less than ten horizontal miles, you can climb from cactus desert into pinyon-juniper woodland, mountain mahogany, ponderosa pine, white fir, aspen, Engelmann spruce, limber pine, bristlecone pine (the oldest living trees), and on above the timberline where the plants are only a few inches tall as in the far northern tundra.

COAL-FIRED POWER?

A long-standing controversy has existed over whether a coal-burning electrical power plant should be built near Cherry Creek. A southern California utility company, constrained by antipollution standards in effect in its home territory, proposed a White Pine solution for generating power with coal transported from mines hundreds of miles to the east in Utah or Wyoming. The Los Angeles Department of Water and Power (LADWP) purchased the Northern Nevada Railway right-of-way from Kennecott on the assumption that this could be arranged. After months of negotiations, the plan was blocked by Senator Harry Reid of Nevada because of environmental concerns. As of 2015, the proposal was in abeyance.

A STATE PRISON

Early in the post-Kennecott era, when White Pine County business leaders searched urgently for new economic incentives, many landed on the idea of a state prison. The overcrowded conditions of the original prison in Carson City forced the government to consider a new venue for a medium-security facility. The state eventually decided on a site in Smith Valley, about 9 miles from Ely. Construction proceeded in two phases in 1988–90 at a cost of more than $54 million.

This addition to the region's economy not only brought new jobs during the construction phase but also a work force of 400

or more employees on a continuing basis for more than twenty-
five years, with the promise that it would continue indefinitely.

Other Towns

Other communities in White Pine bring additional diverse images
into the mosaic. McGill's post Kennecott experience may be told
briefly. It rests on a wide alluvial fan looking westward from the
Schell Creek Mountains. Most of its buildings are neglected and
decaying. Its population had dwindled to about 1,000 in 2015, the
county's more prosperous activity having moved to Ely's closer satellites—the clusters of homes in the Steptoe Valley north, east, and
south of the commercial center.

Another, even sadder story has emerged in Cherry Creek.
It appeared in this narrative earlier as boomtown that tried to
become the county seat in the 1880s. That camp and its artifacts
have long since disappeared. In the early twenty-first century, it
has become, unfortunately, a rural-industrial junkyard, retaining
the debris of two or three generations of contemporary prospectors who have brought their industrial earth-moving hardware
and have left much rusting in place, along with used furniture,
washing machines, tires, and other items not worth taking away.

And finally, the tiny town of Baker near the Utah border
deserves mention. A recent count recorded a population of less
than a hundred, but it sits near the entrance to the Great Basin
National Park. For many years, it has been the home base of environmentalists far and near, advocating for the Park and providing
inspiration for those who resist the transfer of water to the metro-
politan south.

CHAPTER NINE

A Lifeline for the Southeast

Clark's Railroad

REVIVAL IN LINCOLN COUNTY, 1900–1958

The mines in Pioche had been idle for twenty years when the new century opened, and the several Latter-day Saints families of Panaca had gradually adapted to a slower pace in their oasis in upper Meadow Valley. Then the long slumber of the old camp and the Mormon town was roused by the arrival of a railroad.

A millionaire senator from Montana, W. A. Clark, built a connection from Salt Lake City to Los Angeles through the Meadow Valley Wash and Las Vegas Valley in 1903–05. The oasis of Las Vegas had remained a tiny dot on maps after Mormons established a mission there in 1855 and abandoned it three years later. It had become a large ranch operated by the widowed Helen Stewart, still within Lincoln County when the railroad was built.

Suddenly, in 1905, the new town of Las Vegas emerged, a busy whistle stop and maintenance station for the San Pedro, Los Angeles, and Salt Lake Railroad (SP, LA & SL RR)—or "Clark's Salt Lake Line." New residents soon decided they could not tolerate the decadent, debt-ridden county government based in Pioche— 175 miles to the north. So they mounted a movement to establish a new county, named for Senator Clark. "County division" in 1909 was a crucial early step in giving Las Vegas political prominence. At first, voters of Pioche and Panaca resisted county division, but they soon relaxed their opposition; they had little in common with the upstart down in the distant Mojave Desert and were content when newly created Clark County assumed some of their debt.

Pioche's economy gradually revived when local metallurgists found new possibilities in its ores. Also, a spur line from Clark's railroad in Caliente through Panaca to Pioche gave these two towns a new, faster connection to the outside world than their previous links through Utah using animal power.

The long-neglected shafts and mining dumps of Pioche drew prospectors of a new generation. E. H. (Ed) Snyder was a young engineer, born in a neighboring Utah mining camp and trained at the Michigan School of Mines. He did not seek gold and silver ores (although he did not rule them out). Rather, he looked for a method to extract nonprecious minerals, such as lead and zinc, from the lower levels of the old mines. After studying the geology and exploring old mine shafts and dumps, Snyder gathered a few partners and leased properties west of town. From 1915 through 1917, these prospects produced more than $1 million annually. Snyder formed the Combined Metals Reduction Co. (CMR), and in 1923, the company attracted the attention of the National Lead Co., a leading investor in the metals industry, which sponsored his ongoing exploratory work.

The effort languished during the early years of the Great Depression, but in the mid-1930s the Pioche district awakened to the promise of a 170-mile electric power line from Boulder Dam (officially renamed Hoover Dam in 1947) on the Colorado River—200 miles south. When construction was completed in the summer of 1937, the town rejoiced with the largest celebration in its history. The two United States senators, Nevada's congressman, governor, and various other dignitaries arrived for the occasion. Twentieth-century progress had finally reached the most remote region of Nevada.

The district produced and processed ores for two decades. World War II brought a heavy demand for lead and zinc, and the national need continued, to a lesser extent, until the end of the Korean War in 1953. By that time, the ore in the deeper Pioche mines had become more costly to extract and refine. Similar minerals were produced overseas and were more readily available to the market, so prices of raw ore were falling. The original developers ceased most operations in 1958.

Then the old ninety-year-old mining town slumbered a second time. Residents of Pioche and Panaca had cultivated their close relationships in the 1930s, partly because the rejuvenated mines and mill needed many workers who could not all be accommodated on the steep hillsides near the mines. By the 1930s, southern Utah farmers and peddlers could haul their meat and vegetables to Lincoln County by trucks, rather than by team and wagon.

On the strength of the renewed prosperity, the county's voters approved a bond issue for a new courthouse to replace the sixty-five-year-old brick and quartzite edifice that had been the excuse for the fiscal recklessness in the 1870s. The "old courthouse" had been declared unsafe in the 1930s, but it was later stabilized and refurbished with the help of federal and state funds to become a county museum.

The new county governmental center reflected the tastes of the 1930s. It had a white Art Deco exterior, the only courthouse of such design in Nevada. As Ronald James, the historical preservation officer for Nevada wrote, "Art Deco celebrated America's twentieth-century fascination with technology through its stylized ornamentation and structural mass. The Lincoln County Courthouse thus promoted an image of being in step with the rest of the nation in its technological revolution."

One visitor who shared the expectations for a productive future in the region was former President Herbert Hoover, who also had a financial interest in the local mines. He visited in the 1940s, presumably to check on his investments and to evaluate the terrain for further development. Local legend says he spent a night or two at the dilapidated Mountain View Hotel just north of Main Street. But it is more likely that he spent his leisure hours at the home of one of the engineers or executives of the Combined Metals Reduction Company near Caselton, on the other side of the mountain.

CALIENTE

The tiny city of Caliente is three decades younger than Panaca and Pioche, built 125 miles north of Las Vegas in 1901. Though Charles Culverwell had only a few acres under plow and not much outlying land for grazing livestock, a small community had coalesced around his property, known as "Culverwell's." When W. A. Clark's men plotted their first new town in Nevada, they chose the name "Calientes" because of local warm springs. U.S. postal authorities dropped the final "s" two years later.

The Meadow Valley Wash south of Caliente is rugged and narrow for most of its path extending to the Colorado River, a topography that made railroad construction and maintenance difficult. Those who admired this rocky, high-walled crevice called it "Rainbow Canyon." It became a delightful, scenic diversion when passenger trains passed through in the daytime in the early years of the twentieth century. For Clark's construction crews, it was a formidable challenge. They were based at Caliente while they carved and blasted their way southward to lay rails toward Los Angeles.

The wash is a natural funnel that usually carries only a trickle to the Muddy River, 150 miles south. But at times Nature intervenes. Flash floods tormented the railroad builders in the northern part of the Wash three times in the next five years. Raging waters tore out the original railroad tracks for a hundred miles. In 1910, no through traffic moved for six months.

Such frequent and extensive maintenance required manpower. Most men on the work crews got room and board in Caliente. In the 1910 U.S. census, Caliente had a population 1,755; Las Vegas had 945. Because Caliente was a stop along Clark's line, the SP, LA & SL established a maintenance station there. His crews built a depot and a row of sturdy cottages, portending a bright future. They also constructed the branch line 25 miles north to Pioche to tap its mineral resources. In the early 1920s, after Senator Clark sold his interest to the Union Pacific, the new owner transferred a major part of its maintenance operation from Las Vegas to Caliente.

One of the attractive improvements of the UP in Caliente was a substantial Mission Revival depot to serve railroad passengers. For decades, it was one of the most widely admired structures in the region. Caliente continued to be an important maintenance point for a quarter century. Passenger trains stopped there and offered convenient service to locals who wanted to travel to Utah, Las Vegas, or southern California. The rail yards also received ores from Pioche and routed them northward to smelters in Utah. During World War II, as diesel locomotives replaced steam engines, this strategic advantage declined.

The tiny "city" endures more than a century after its founding, little changed since the days of Senator Clark's town planners. The handsome depot served as a museum for a few years, before the decline resumed. Because of its benign climate, it calls itself the "Rose City of the Silver State."

PAHRANAGAT VALLEY AND ALAMO

Pahranagat first appeared on the Nevada and American agenda in the early 1860s because of a hoax. Journalists writing for the *Territorial Enterprise* of Virginia City, such as Mark Twain and Dan DeQuille, were accustomed to filling their newspaper columns with manufactured sensations. The basic points of the story did not have to be true—quite the contrary. But there needed to be enough seeming authenticity to trick the reader into accepting a fantasy.

Dan DeQuille published a satirical piece about mysterious "traveling stones" in the Pahranagat Mountains, "the wildest and most sterile part of southeastern Nevada." According to this account, a prospector in that remote area had brought back several perfectly round, heavy stones. When placed two or three feet apart upon a level surface like a floor or tabletop, they moved toward a common center and then "huddled up in a bunch like a lot of eggs in a nest."

DeQuille's tall tale caught fire in the gullible media of the day. It was widely repeated and republished in the East and, as the legends tell us, even in Europe. The tale was probably intended as a comic metaphor for the mining rushes occurring across Nevada at the time. The facts about the region are more prosaic.

Mormons explored the Pahranagat Valley as early as 1858, when it was visited by an expedition searching for a possible hiding place for church leaders in case of a resumption of the Mormon War. Native Americans were cultivating crops along the banks of the stream at that time. "Pahranagat" is thought to be a Southern Paiute term for "squash."

A few Anglo farmers settled on the fertile acres in the mid-1860s, at the time of the mining rush to Irish Mountain. The town of Hiko, about 8 miles east of the mines, grew up around the mill because water was available, and the land could be irrigated and cultivated. Contemporary accounts from the 1860s (which are suspect) assert that several hundred people made homes in the vicinity during the brief Irish Mountain boom. Historian John

Townley, in his booklet *Conquered Provinces*, playfully called Hiko "the Metropolis of Pahranagat Valley."

Before 1900, Pahranagat seemed to offer more possibilities for community development than Las Vegas. It was a verdant oasis extending from about 70 to 100 miles north of the place where Helen Stewart had her La Vegas ranch. In its center, the valley is 30 miles long and about one-half to two miles wide, and its soil produces an abundance of natural grass for livestock. According to local lore, it was a favorite place for horse thieves to hide their illicit bounty in the nineteenth century.

The town of Alamo was a younger, distant cousin of other LDS communities in southern Utah and Nevada. Founded in 1905–06, it put a distinctively Mormon stamp on Pahranagat Valley soon after the turn of the century.

Alamo was named for cottonwood trees that grew near the water. It was founded even while its distant neighbor Delamar was fading as a gold camp. Much moveable property, including lumber from houses, was available for bargain prices. The valley had plenty of water and a long growing season, so it was suitable for the industrious LDS settlers.

While the families arriving from Mormon country in the first decade of the twentieth century did not come as an organized community, this village evolved into a semicooperative LDS village to meet common needs. Pahranagat Valley Mormons sought self-sufficiency in most essential food products. Until the appearance of television in the 1950s, cultural services were also mostly homegrown and centered on church activities. Children who grew up there occasionally attended the Lincoln County High School in Panaca, 60 miles away, before a local high school was established in the 1930s.

But during the later years of the twentieth century, this quiet region on the wide fringe between the Great Basin and Mojave deserts became a vast arena of Cold War conflict. It was a village neighbor to the Nevada Test Site, where nuclear weapon experiments were conducted for more than forty years.

CHAPTER TEN

The MX Missile Controversy, 1978–81, and the Thirty-Five-Year Water War, 1980–2015

THE MX MISSILE CONTROVERSY

In the late 1970s, a passionate public debate enflamed Nevada politics. It concerned a proposal to turn the state's southeastern desert into a potential war zone. This was the grotesque proposal by the U.S. Air Force to install 200 missiles in silos there, each capable of delivering ten nuclear warheads to targets in Soviet Russia. It was called Missile Experimental, or MX. This sprawling cluster of deadly weapons would have been based mostly in Lincoln, Nye, and White Pine counties, plus parts of southwestern Utah. The main operational center would be located north of Las Vegas. A "racetrack" labyrinth would permit rapid and frequent shuttling of the missiles among the silos in order to evade Soviet targeting. Cost estimates ranged from $30 to $60 billion. If the missiles had been installed as planned, they would have permanently changed the high desert and Mojave landscapes.

The proposal generated several long seasons of publicity and dozens of public hearings. The more information Nevadans received about the scheme, the more firmly opposed most of them became. The controversy continued for more than three years in the late 1970s and early 1980s, during the last half of the presidency of Jimmy Carter and into the administration of Ronald Reagan. When residents of Nevada's rural counties were given a chance to vote on the plan in a referendum, they registered overwhelming opposition. Early in his first term, President Reagan abandoned the project, and most Nevadans living in the North-Center rejoiced at their reprieve.

During these years, the remote regions of rural southeastern Nevada received more attention than ever before. Geologists, hydrologists, archeologists, sociologists, and volunteers appeared on the landscape like swarms of crickets.

It was the hydrologists who also generated the next large controversy. For the first time, most Nevadans regarded the zone where the high desert of the Great Basin blends with the Mojave a resource for its beauty, its delicate ecology, and the unique cultural virtues it offered to residents and outsiders. But the zone also also offered formerly unknown temptations to the dwellers of the Mojave.

A Water War in the Southeast

Nothing provokes a fight in desert country like a water-rights dispute. Many quarrels over mining claims were settled quickly by gunfire or by a rush to the local courthouse, but water claims more often have a life span of many decades. Without intending to do so, the promoters of deep-well pumping for military uses set the stage for proposals that might fill the swimming pools of Las Vegas but to the permanent disadvantage of eastern Nevada.

Long after the memories of the MX fantasy had faded, White Pine and Lincoln counties faced another ominous threat. This challenge arose over the potential water resources in the mountains and beneath the valleys of the Great Basin high country—the lifeblood of the region's land and culture. Las Vegas valley water managers examined the hydrological data the MX planners had developed and decided they could tap these sources.

The dazzling story of southern Nevada's economic expansion has often been retold. Within three decades, Las Vegas evolved from a railroad water stop to an international tourist destination. It offered extravagant gambling halls and show venues, swimming pools and spas, golf courses and abundant greenery, defying the aridity and heat of the desert.

The census of 1940 counted about 16,000 people in Clark County; in 1990, the number was 741,000; in 2000 it was 1,375,000; and by 2010 nearly two million. The casino business and military operations such as Nellis Air Force Base and the Nevada Test Site boosted the population by tens of thousands each year. Water needs grew accordingly.

Farther north, the population of the rural counties remained stable over the decades—about 10,000 for White Pine and 4,000 or 5,000 for Lincoln. In addition, a few hundred people lived in the northeastern corner of Nye County. Most natural watersheds in these areas trend southward toward the Mojave, before they disappear or trickle underground into the Colorado River basin. It was these delicate streams and the potential deep aquifers beneath them that attracted the attention of Las Vegas water managers.

In the last quarter of the twentieth century, managers of the Las Vegas Valley Water District (LVVWD) claimed that their metropolis was in danger of running dry. Early residents of the railroad-city era had pumped the local aquifer down to a dangerously low level. But when Hoover Dam was constructed during the 1930s, the thirsty valley had the promise of a solution. A portion of the Colorado River was available to Nevada because of the Colorado River Compact ratified by Congress in the 1920s. Over the next sixty years or more, as that water was pumped and piped through the Las Vegas valley, it was the elixir for growth. Yet, as the city continued its outward sprawl, planners began to want even more.

The threat to Lincoln, White Pine, and Nye counties arose gradually and was only gradually understood. In the last two or three decades of the twentieth century, when the mining and livestock businesses were shrinking in the high country, Las Vegas experienced the most robust period of urban growth in the nation. New casinos, housing developments, lavish lawns, fountains, and swimming pools proliferated in an area in the Mojave where the desert sun often raises the temperatures above 110 degrees Fahrenheit. As the need for water in Las Vegas accelerated, Nevada's legally allotted share of water from the Colorado River seemed less than adequate to LVVWD authorities. In 1989, they filed 147 applications to import water from thirty different valleys north of Clark County.

Meanwhile, Las Vegas was wasting much of the water it imported from the Colorado River. The Nevada Division of Environmental Protection (NDEP), in a survey conducted during the 1990s, concluded that Las Vegas Valley water users were consuming 316 gallons per person per day, compared with 281 in Reno, 209 in Phoenix, and 158 in Tucson. Passionate objections to the plan to pipe the water from the northern counties came from many directions.

In 1993, LVVWD withdrew some of its applications from the state engineer's office and changed its emphasis. It sought more water from Arizona and California and reorganized itself as the Southern Nevada Water Authority (SNWA) representing a broader coalition of Clark County clients. In 2004, Nevada's Congressional delegation, led by Senator Harry Reid, managed to pass a law called the Lincoln County Conservation, Recreation, and Development Act.

This measure granted a right-of-way to SNWA to transfer appropriated water—an amount equal to a medium-sized river, if one had existed in Nevada—from the northern valleys of Lincoln and Nye counties in exchange for promised investments in environmental protection and recreational facilities to encourage tourism. It was an obscure bargain, but it encouraged SNWA and their agents to resume their efforts to buy ranches with water rights in the northern regions. In Lincoln County, the county commissioners and some ranchers initially agreed to the arrangement but later reconsidered. In White Pine, local government opposition was quick to oppose and continued to be tenacious in 2015.

When SNWA tried to revive some of the 1989 filings more than fifteen years later, and the Office of the State Engineer resumed its notices to ranchers and other owners, a network of environmentalists challenged the process in court and won a landmark case in the Nevada Supreme Court (*Great Basin Water Network v. Taylor*, 2010). The court ruled that the State Engineer could not simply renotice the property owners of 1993 but must begin the entire process a second time to give the current owners a reasonable opportunity to respond. By 2015, battle over the northern water had become a David-and-Goliath struggle. The giant from the south had the big business advantages: money and political clout.

At least five valleys in Nevada—Spring, White River, Delamar, Cave, and Dry Lake—were threatened, as well as fifteen basins and the adjacent mountain ranges and Utah counties sharing the aquifers. Of particular interest to all parties was Spring Valley, which stretches for a hundred miles adjacent to the Snake Range, part of which holds the Great Basin National Park and a nationally designated wilderness area at Mt. Moriah.

The impact of such a massive water transfer on these resources raised alarms among many groups. In 2006, a coalition of private citizens founded the Great Basin Water Network (GBNW), which mobilized thousands of allies. When the Nevada State Engineer proposed to authorize the transfer of 800,000 acre-feet per year, the GBWN filed suit to block such a huge transfer, and won a partial victory in court.

The Bureau of Land Management also opposed the transfer because it is custodian and caretaker of federal public lands. In addition, one of the largest landholders and water rights owners in northern Spring Valley was the Mormon Church, owner of the former Cleveland Ranch. The church had its own agenda. It raised rangeland products for its worldwide food distribution services to needy people. In 2011, the LDS Church joined the opposition. In 2013, the governor of Utah also registered objections to the proposed compromise because of its effect on neighboring Utah basins.

In addition to the impact that such a vast drawdown of the Great Basin aquifer might have on traditional community life, ranching, and recreational activities, there were many questions about its effect on ecology and wildlife. The U.S. government has established several areas to protect endangered species of fish and unique plants that exist only in this region. Several small lakes furnish resting and feeding places for migrating birds. Such oases would undoubtedly be damaged.

Las Vegas was making another wager on its future, a daring bet that if it invested billions of dollars of borrowed money on a pumping and pipeline system, it could develop enough water resources in the semi-arid northern valleys to slake the thirst of Las Vegas Valley for another decade or two.

For many of the participants in this dispute, the memories of the transfer of Owens Valley water, high in the Sierra, to Los Angeles early in the twentieth century became a familiar touchstone. Owens Valley never recovered from the shift of its most precious resource to the southern desert.

Many questions on the projected water transfer lingered into the second decade of the twenty-first century. Does the Las Vegas valley actually need the amount of water that is expected from the northern valleys if it seriously conserves what it has already imported? Does the recession of the years 2008–13 suggest that Clark County might not sustain the population increases of the previous forty years?

Las Vegas valley water authorities have reported many successful efforts to conserve and recycle available water. In 2015, John Entsminger, general manager of SNWA, assured a governor's conference that the area has enough water to allow for growth for the next forty years with present arrangements in place. If so, this would make the pipeline unnecessary.

Experts have tried many times to estimate the cost of the project. In the 1990s, their guesses ranged from $4.5 to $7.5 billion for construction and financing. Twenty years later, some estimates were at least double that amount. The long-running drama in the southeast corner of the Mosaic is still unfolding.

CHAPTER ELEVEN

Lovelock, Winnemucca, and Battle Mountain Revisited

For the first thirty years after their founding, Lovelock, Winnemucca, and Battle Mountain were little more than tiny beads on the Central Pacific Railroad necklace. The census of 1900 counted slightly more than a thousand residents in the first two of these places and another 365 in Battle Mountain—about 2,500 souls in about 20,000 square miles.

LOVELOCK, PART TWO

If an impartial observer who had visited all the towns of the North-Center in 1900 had been asked to identify the community with the best prospects for the future, he might have chosen Lovelock. Historian John Townley, describing the Great Basin at that period, dubbed this place the "Cinderella town" of the Humboldt region. While it did not rise to this expectation as the twentieth century unfolded, it held its own as one of the most stable small communities in the area.

Allen C. Bragg, editor of the Winnemucca newspaper, the *Silver State*, spent a few days here in 1905 and found it to be one of the prettiest and most promising villages in the state: "Lovelock is 'on the trail' to be a city of considerable magnitude. If I could come back to this dusty ball 50 years hence I should see a city of at least 50,000 souls, for Lovelock Valley, if put to its highest uses would support 50,000 or 75,000 busy men and women and it would be an ideal spot to raise children and start them in life with bright prospects."

There was a widespread view a century ago that Nevada's valleys had rich soil, which could be made productive if water resources could be found. The Big Meadows offered superficial confirmation of this fantasy. It is longer and wider than the Truckee Meadows, where Reno and Sparks are located, and a larger natural platform than those occupied by Elko and Winnemucca. But in its 150-year history, the Lovelock area has experienced a slower transition than any of its relatives along the Truckee–Humboldt route. The census counted 3,103 residents in Pershing County in 1950 and about 6,753 in 2010.

When Pershing County was established in 1919, Lovelock took its new status as a county seat seriously. It engaged Frederick DeLongchamps, Nevada's most creative and prolific architect, and invited him to provide a distinctive courthouse design. The result was a round building sitting on a hexagonal foundation, including a circular courtroom. Its design, based on the Jefferson library at the University of Virginia, holds a special place in U.S. public buildings for local government. It is situated not on the central commercial street but a city block away in a spacious sward of grass and trees. The county has had nearly a century of service from this innovative structure.

The farmers of the Big Meadows gained more stability after 1936 because of the Rye Patch Dam, located on the Humboldt River 22 miles upstream from Lovelock. Built by the U.S. Bureau of Reclamation, it tries to assure irrigation water in dry periods and protection against flood when the river flows too rapidly. The reservoir is 20 miles long, allowing recreational possibilities at places designed for fishing, boating, and picnics.

As of 2010, Pershing County had nearly a quarter-million acres planted in crops, with 135 farms averaging about 1,800 acres each. The main product was alfalfa, alfalfa seed, and other types of hay, much of which was shipped to out-of-state markets. Livestock owners counted more than 23,000 animals. In addition, the county shared a portion of the gold-mining prosperity farther east along the Humboldt River corridor.

WINNEMUCCA, PART TWO

While Humboldt County had been a center for woman suffrage advocacy during the 1870s, a hotbed for the silver crusade in the 1890s, and a chosen place for Sarah Winnemucca's experimental school for Paiute children, these were brief episodes in the cultural life of the region. Most of its residents were trying to coax a living along the banks of the river or from a few scattered mines and ranches. Yet two young men who passed through Winnemucca late in the nineteenth century managed to use it as a springboard into politics and finance at state and national levels.

As the twentieth century opened, Nevada's two seats in the United States Senate were still held by oligarchs who had begun their careers on the Comstock Lode in the earliest years of statehood. Senators William M. Stewart and John P. Jones had been repeatedly re-elected by the state legislature, many of whose members were puppets of the Central Pacific railroad. The pattern was finally interrupted when these two retired, Jones in 1903 and Stewart in 1905. A new century brought new players into the political game.

By 1900, Winnemucca had become the hometown of a new pair of protopoliticians who, by chance, built the social networks that replaced the old guard of the Comstock era. George Wingfield, a cowboy-gambler partnered with George Nixon, and together they parlayed their modest Humboldt county beginnings into state and national prominence.

Nixon, whom we met earlier as a banker, editor, and Silver Party leader, had been a telegraph operator in Winnemucca in the early 1880s before he organized a bank and became the owner of the *Silver State*, the local newspaper, in 1890. His advocacy on behalf of the Silver Party in the 1890s opened a gateway into politics at the state level. After 1900, when he left Winnemucca to join the rush to Tonopah and Goldfield, he already had a statewide reputation. His mining investments paid off better in the southern camps than in Winnemucca. In 1905, the legislature elected him U.S. Senator to replace Stewart. Nixon held this office until his death in 1913.

His friend George Wingfield had a less exalted beginning but a longer career on Nevada's economic stage. He had grown up on cattle ranches in the Lakeview region of southeastern Oregon. As a young cowboy herding livestock more than 200 miles to the railroad at Winnemucca, he liked what he found there and stayed. He became a successful gambler, a skillful poker player.

While Wingfield spent only a few years in Winnemucca, it was time enough to accumulate some cash and business acumen. He invested and lost money in the newly opened copper mines at Golconda about 16 miles east of Winnemucca, but his winnings from saloons and gambling tables eased the pain of that failure.

Like Nixon, Wingfield followed the early mining rush to Goldfield. When Nixon died, some legislators offered him an appointment to the vacant U.S. Senate seat, but he declined, preferring to give his attentions to the Goldfield mining operations. As those enterprises faded, he became the baron of the northern Nevada banking business during the 1920s. He loaned much money to ranchers and miners. When his banks collapsed during financial panic of 1933, he and those who had invested in his financial empire lost their deposits, which most of them never recovered. He had owned banks in Winnemucca, Elko, and Wells, among other places.

While Nixon had built an opera house in Winnemucca, later used as a community center, Wingfield was little remembered in the Humboldt region. In downtown Reno, Wingfield Park is a reminder of his influence and municipal largess.

One the most frequently articulated hopes among Winnemucca businessmen of the mid-twentieth century was that the city might become the inland hub for a new highway directed into Oregon and eventually to the Pacific Ocean, promoted as the "Winnemucca to the Sea" route. Its leading advocate was Fritz Buckingham, a resident of Paradise Valley. The proposed route would have passed through Lakeview and Klamath Falls, Oregon, eventually reaching Crescent City, California. Buckingham generated interest among businessmen in southern Oregon towns, and was elected to the Nevada legislature three times, serving in four sessions (1957 through 1963).

In the end, little benefit came to Humboldt County from these efforts. Interstate 80 and the railroads could carry vehicles and freight to the heart of northern California through Reno much more rapidly than the twisted route that Buckingham and his allies advocated.

Though the ambitious alternate highway project was a disappointment, another, more mundane enterprise—raising potatoes in the broad valleys of the north—brought rewards to those who experimented with it. The high Basin terrain, which discouraged many other crops, proved to be excellent soil for the spud. A large food-distribution company opened a plant in Winnemucca for dehydrating and shipping the tubers to markets across the nation.

Humboldt County continued to be one of the leading producers of alfalfa and related products in the state, with more than 50,000 acres under cultivation. And Winnemucca's economy continued to be supported by railroad and livestock businesses. More recently, gold mining has become increasingly important. In 2009, gold producers employed more than a thousand workers.

Buckaroo Hall of Fame

Like many communities in the far West, Winnemucca promotes its heritage as a livestock-producing center. It is home to the Buckaroo Hall of Fame, founded in 1989. The founders rejected the title of "cowboy," believing the term had become associated with the "rhinestone," white-hat pretenders generated by Hollywood. "Working cattlemen and horsemen" are honored here.

Its museum is the venue for the William B. Humphrey's Big Game collection, featuring more than fifty animals from around the world.

Battle Mountain, Part Two

For more than a century after its founding, the town of Battle Mountain had a less obvious presence in Nevada politics than its nearest neighbors—Winnemucca, Elko, and Austin. It was not a county seat until 1979, when Lander County voters finally withdrew that privilege from Austin. Battle Mountain was less important to the Central/Southern Pacific than other towns along the route but more promising than its southern neighbor 90 miles away. Although nearby mines were thought to have a variety of ores, none left records of significant output in the first hundred years.

Battle Mountain added population gradually during the twentieth century, while Austin languished. U.S. Highway 40 and the transcontinental railroad business continued to provide economic nourishment. By 1940, the railroad town had more than 1,100 residents; its southern rival had fewer than 600. After the 1950s, Battle Mountain also received commercial energy from Interstate 80.

Austin finally lost the game when the Nevada legislature authorized a ballot, and the northern voters won by a large margin. Part of the transition required establishing a courthouse in Battle Mountain without incurring large expense. The county commissioners selected a former schoolhouse and remodeled it to reflect the neoclassical style of most other Nevada courthouses built in the early twentieth century.

Lander County and Battle Mountain took a large leap into the twenty-first century with an innovative new courthouse south of town on the Austin highway. Its architectural design breaks completely with the past, abandoning the traditional classical facade. Within its glass entrance is a three-story-high montage of photographs of the early history of the region.

Battle Mountain gained its new status just as the gold bonanza of the late twentieth century was emerging in Elko and Eureka counties, and it shared much of the bounty. Lander County's gold production in recent years has been substantial but less impressive than the output of its eastern neighbors. Its population in 2010 was almost exactly the same as ten years earlier—5,775. But, if one makes local inquiries, the estimates are higher.

One of the best-publicized annual events for attracting visitors to Battle Mountain is the Off-Highway Vehicle (OHV) gathering in late summer. The town invites owners of dirt bikes, four-wheelers, and human-powered machines to test their skills and vehicles in designated areas south of I-80 where they can "get away from it all, yet see it all" in mountainous terrain covered with pinyon, juniper, and sagebrush. Riders are advised not to disturb the wildlife or terrain as they race their vehicles.

CHAPTER TWELVE

New Agendas for Elko County

Tourism, Entertainment, Gold

During the first century in the recorded history of the upper Humboldt region, mining was only a small factor. The region had no boom camps comparable to those farther south in Lincoln and White Pine, or in other parts of the state. But the Elko–Carlin region rewrote that scenario in the last half of the twentieth century. Nevada's latest mining boom began here, has lasted much longer, and has made all the earlier boomtowns seem miniscule by comparison.

The census of 1900 counted 5,688 residents in the 17,000 square miles of Elko County, with only 849 living in the town of Elko. Those settlers who had made their homes in this corner of the Great Basin were mostly ranchers or families whose men were working on the railroad.

The economy along the upper Humboldt got a boost in 1909–10 when the Western Pacific Railroad (WPRR) built a second line across the Basin approximately parallel to the existing Southern Pacific rails. George Gould, one of the railroad barons of the time, was eager to challenge the fabled Central Pacific route (which had been absorbed into the SPRR) and Clark's line to southern California. The WPRR began to lay tracks on a more direct route from Utah to California than the old Central Pacific had chosen; it entered the state at Wendover and crossed into California near Beckworth Pass about 15 miles northwest of Reno. This route offered fewer construction challenges than the one selected by Crocker for the CP over Donner Summit in the 1860s.

The project gave Elko and other towns along the upper Humboldt River a second surge, almost exactly thirty years after their founding by the Central Pacific. For more than 120 miles, the WP tracks ran parallel to those of the SP along the gradual gradient of the river. West of Winnemucca the WP left the Humboldt and took a more direct route to California across the Black Rock Desert.

Initially, the relationship between the WP and the SP executives was tense, but eventually the two agreed to cooperate in sharing their tracks—both companies using one track for westbound trains and the other for eastbound traffic. This arrangement was in effect for many years. While the new era of railroad building was much less consequential than that of 1869, it brought new commercial possibilities from Elko County all the way to Winnemucca.

Tourism and Entertainment

During the 1920s and 1930s, Elko gradually became aware of its possibilities for attracting tourists. Its outdoor recreation options expanded as the automobile became a common family vehicle and as the governments provided paved highways. A necessary addition was comfortable hotels or motor lodges for the travelers.

The couple who initiated the new standard for northern Nevada was Newton and Lee Crumley. They had operated businesses in Tonopah and Goldfield in the 1920s before moving to Elko, where they purchased the old Commercial Hotel. Their establishment dispensed interesting food and drinks and catered to short-time visitors, who became more numerous as automobile traffic increased.

One of his early clients was the Hollywood star Bing Crosby, who first visited Elko in about 1942, generated publicity, and soon bought a cattle ranch. Crosby, then one of America's most popular singers and actors, was trying to escape the glitter and pressures of stardom. He sought not only a rustic retreat from southern California but also the authentic life of a working rancher.

Crosby later bought more ranches in Elko County and regularly brought his wife and sons so they could benefit from the cowboy experience. He became Elko's most famous visitor-celebrity, designated an honorary mayor of the city. He introduced several other Hollywood personalities to the region and endeared himself to local residents by offering free performances and making generous gifts to local charities.

Another citizen important in anticipating Nevada's tourist business in the 1940s was John E. Robbins, who represented Elko County in the state senate from 1935 until 1953. He was locally known as "the father of Nevada gambling law" because of his role in shaping legislation enacted in 1945 that provided for the regulation and taxation of the gaming business by the state government.

Elko sits about in the center of the Great Basin, roughly halfway between the Wasatch Mountains and the Sierra Nevada. In the north-south directions, no other city challenges its primacy between Boise and Las Vegas. And while Elko has never been a serious competitor to Las Vegas, Reno, or Lake Tahoe as a gambling and entertainment center, it has been the leading venue for such attractions in the North-Center. In addition, its primary distinction for the last half century has been the pursuit of prosperity through Nevada's original quest—the search for and production of gold.

GOLD MINING SINCE 1965

In the mid-1960s, gold mining appeared to be a dormant industry in the West, a relic of a fading era. A booklet published by Professor Albin B. Dahl of the University of Nevada Bureau of Business Research in May 1964 reported that gold was being produced primarily as "the ancillary product of lead, zinc and silver mines": "The State has been thoroughly prospected for bodies of ore capable of producing gold on a commercially profitable basis, given the current fixed price other metal. Apparently there is little promise of new opportunities in gold production by underground mining methods."

But below the radar of the macroeconomists, traditional prospectors were still probing mountains that had long been considered barren. As early as 1955, a Battle Mountain miner, Marion Fisher, and his associates identified gold-bearing ore near the Humboldt River in the vicinity of Carlin, but the precious metal in this area was so widely dispersed it had escaped the attention of traditional prospectors. Earlier generations of diggers had found promising rocks, crushed them with a mortar and pestle, washed the product, and carried samples into an assay office. The kind of deposit that Fisher identified defied such analysis, for it required microscopic examination.

Several years passed before international mining companies became interested. By the 1980s, Newmont Mining Co., one of the giants of the industry, had bought out the discoverers. Other large firms also invested in prospects along the Humboldt Basin. This section of Nevada, which had previously recorded only tiny amounts of "yellow metal," eventually became the primary American source of newly mined gold.

In the thirty-five years between 1980 and 2015, Elko/Carlin was the hub of one of the richest gold producing areas in the world. The rising price, the availability of huge earth-moving equipment, and advanced chemical procedures for leaching the gold from the native rock enabled investors to extract ore at greater profit than ever before. Because of this activity, the economic recession of 2008–11 did little damage to northeastern Nevada. And while the Las Vegas tourism and real estate markets spiraled downward, the same kind of businesses along the upper Humboldt corridor held their own. Early in the so-called "Great Recession," Elko and its nearest neighbors were enjoying a surge of activity that the *Wall Street Journal* called a "Gold-Plated Economy": "Gold fever has inoculated this historic cow town from the state's economic malaise, making it an island of relative prosperity in a state flooded with unemployed workers."

Visitors to Elko in the second decade of the twenty-first century could get a richer variety of impressions of the North-Center than could be found anywhere else in the state. It was still a railroad town promoting its cowboy heritage and tastefully celebrating the memories of the past 150 years. Its ornate, neoclassical courthouse, built early in the last century with the traditional columns, dome, and balustrade remains the most impressive building in center of the city, not a relic among skyscrapers. It is still in service a century after its dedication, a symbol of the county's conservative traditions. The city's main thoroughfare, Idaho Street, rumbles and roars with huge trucks, carrying their cargo and spewing their exhaust into the fresh high desert air, where it usually dissipates quickly.

It almost seemed that the national economic recession of 2008–11 helped Elko. With instability in the world currency markets, gold prices seemed to be a good bet. At its peak, the price of gold hovered at about $1,800 per ounce, and with the promise of more and deeper mining, there seemed to be no end to the blue skies. But gold prices, like silver in the 1870s, fluctuate, and by 2015, they had lost some of their luster.

Never had Nevadans seen a more robust mining boom. And never before has so much of the profit from the mineral wealth been carried off to distant banks. Nevada's constitution allows mining companies to pay property taxes only on the net proceeds, that is, the profits they report on ore production. In the decades since this provision was embedded in the state constitution, mining companies have found ways to take most of their profits in other states or countries, rather than in the jurisdiction where it was extracted.

Another peculiarity of the Nevada law assures that a substantial part of the mining taxes collected goes into the treasuries of the counties where the ore was mined. While Elko is the commercial and cultural center of the region, most of the ore is mined in mountains west of the city—in Eureka, Lander, and Humboldt counties. Thus, a relatively modest amount of the local mining tax revenue was received in Elko. Also, relatively little of the net tax proceeds reached the state treasury. In several other western states, a severance tax channels more of the revenue into state treasuries.

Libraries

Elko's book-loving community created the first public collection of reading material in 1922 and began immediately to catalog it for public use. Its members persevered in gathering and lending books while moving from a borrowed room in the courthouse to temporary quarters in a former high school building. There, a fire destroyed many of their resources in 1942. The community resumed its efforts in a rented lodge hall; improved public and private financing enabled it to occupy a new building in 1974. In the meantime, Elko's librarians had begun to offer services to patrons in Eureka and Lander counties as well as borrowers in the scattered expanse of Elko County by bookmobiles.

GREAT BASIN COLLEGE

Elko has broken new ground in expanding educational opportunities for students three times during its century-and-a-half history. First, it was the home of the so-called University Preparatory School from 1874 until 1885, before the school was moved to Reno. Second, in 1895 it became the first county in the state to establish a high school. And third, it led the way in the community college movement in the 1960s, although Nevada as a whole was the last state in the nation to initiate this level of instruction.

Business leaders in Elko promoted the idea of such an institution as early as the 1950s, but the state Board of Regents and its administrators resisted the idea; their meager funds were inadequate to serve the needs of the University of Nevada in Reno (opened in 1886) and its younger counterpart in Las Vegas (which began awarding degrees in 1964). Nevada had one of the weakest financial foundations for higher education in the nation. The concept of a community college in a rural area had to wait until the later 1960s, when Elko resurrected it.

At that time, generous local donors enabled the school board to hire a community college director from Oregon in 1967. Governor Paul Laxalt, who, as the son of a Basque sheepherder, had a fondness for the Nevada rangelands, became a crucial supporter of the movement in Carson City. The embryonic institution struggled to stay alive for the first year, but in 1968, it received an unexpected gift of $250,000 from the industrialist-financier Howard Hughes, who late in life became a recluse in a Las Vegas hotel. This donation, together with additional support from the state superintendent of public instruction in Carson City, gave the College the resources it needed to survive in its most vulnerable early years. In 1969, the Nevada legislature granted the first state funding and assigned responsibility for governing the College to the Board of Regents of the University of Nevada.

This educational infant of questionable birth initially called itself Elko Community College. Later it became Northern Nevada Community College, and eventually, as its mission expanded,

Great Basin College. By 2010, it had branches in Winnemucca, Ely, Battle Mountain, and as far away as Pahrump in southern Nye County. Later, its outreach extended to Mineral and Esmeralda counties. The recession of 2008–11 sharply reduced revenue from the state government, but the College was trying to close the gaps in its teaching and service by using electronic alternatives to classroom teaching. The mining companies have also been supportive.

THE NORTHEASTERN NEVADA MUSEUM

No county in the state devoted more resources per capita to the preservation and tasteful display of its local history than Elko. A group of the county's citizens began gathering artifacts and oral history in 1956. With the help of the city government, the Fleischmann Foundation of Nevada, the Nevada State Museum, and a broad spectrum of local contributors, they organized the Northeastern Nevada Historical Society, opening the doors of a small museum in 1968.

When the Society hired Howard Hickson, who had previously been in charge of exhibits at the Nevada State Museum in Carson City, it took a crucial step in expansion. Hickson served as director from 1969 to 1993, applying his artistic skills not only to displaying artifacts but to launch the *Northeastern Nevada Historical Society Quarterly*, a publication devoted to research and distribution of information about the region's past.

Meanwhile, the museum expanded its resources in the preservation of regional history. It acquired the remains of a Pony Express cabin built in the 1860s from Ruby Valley, brought it to Elko, and restored it on the Museum grounds. Chief Justice Earl Warren of the U.S. Supreme Court delivered the dedicatory speech.

Hickson and the Society's active board gradually expanded the financial base and attracted attention far beyond Elko. H.V. (Jack) Wanamaker of Burbank, California, saw the museum and decided it was an appropriate place to display his collection of carefully preserved big game animals. He donated not only his collection of more than fifty specimens but also $1 million toward the construction of a new wing for the museum. The wing was dedicated in 1999. By 2010, its 40,000-square feet were attracting about

30,000 visitors each year. The Wiegand Foundation of Nevada has also been helpful, financially and otherwise, to this and other museums in the region.

Cowboy Poetry and the Western Folklife Center

Elko has also become a regionally known venue for cowboy poetry. From 1985, when the first meeting of rhyming wranglers gathered to share stories and poems, the event evolved into an annual January event with a much broader scope.

In its earliest years, the event was designed primarily for cowboys and their fans who had few responsibilities on the range in midwinter. It brought a few hundred ropers and herders from across the far West. Elko can be bitterly cold in the first month of the year, but that does not deter bards of the rangelands from gathering. The event has also become a significant draw for tourists and gained some international promise in 1990 when a significant number of Australian rhymers participated.

During the following decade, George Gund, a Midwestern and San Francisco businessman, purchased one of Elko's older hotels and remodeled it as the Western Folklife Center, an expansion of the cowboy poetry idea. This became a depository for memorabilia and a meeting place that opens its facilities to the public throughout the year. It has evolved into a regional resource, offering its services to much of the far West.

California Trail Interpretive Center

Twelve miles west of Elko on a low ridge overlooking I-80 and the Humboldt River sits one of Nevada's newest museums. It is dedicated to the rich history of the explorers and pioneers who crossed the western half of North America between 1841 and 1869—the years of the first emigrants and completion of the first transcontinental railroad. The California Trail Interpretive Center was dedicated in 2008.

It is the result of collaboration between local, state, and federal governments, supplemented by generous gifts from local donors. It is a spacious and well-designed edifice, and the grounds are rich with statues and markers commemorating the pioneers.

A SAMPLING OF ELKO'S OTHER COMMUNITIES: SPRING CREEK, CARLIN, WELLS, WEST WENDOVER, AND JACKPOT

A relatively young addition to the roster of communities is Spring Creek, six miles southeast of Elko on the road toward Lamoille Canyon in the Ruby Mountains. Initially planned in the 1970s, the area soon became attractive to people seeking homes beyond the traditional city but nearby. The addition of local schools, a golf course, and facilities for horses added to its appeal. Its population expanded from 5,886 in 1990 to 12,361 in 2010. It acquired the amenities of a prosperous suburb as the gold boom expanded.

Elko's two original Central Pacific neighbors, Carlin and Wells, did not have as many opportunities for community development as the county seat. Although the railroad built stations at both places, the head start that Elko received with its local government offices was decisive. Carlin was expected to benefit from its potential connection northward to the mining town of Tuscarora. In Wells, the surrounding springs offered promising pasture for livestock, but neither town flourished. Serious fires stunted the early development of Wells three times in its first thirty years.

There was much speculation over the decades about a rail connection between Wells and Twin Falls, Idaho, with the Union Pacific as the investor, but this was not realized until 1926.

In February 2008, many older buildings in Wells were badly damaged by a magnitude 6.0 earthquake, whose epicenter was only a few miles distant. This was another reminder—if any were needed—of the fragility of the earth's crust in many parts of the Basin. This small town remains another of Nevada's tenacious outposts in a challenging environment.

Fifty-nine miles east of Wells is the flashy complex of West Wendover, which has no reason to exist except its proximity to the Utah state line on I-80. Only a dozen people lived there at the western edge of the Bonneville Salt Flat in the early 1940s. But when the U.S. Army Air Forces established an air base and training school for the crews of World War II bombers near Wendover, Utah, the obscure Nevada satellite got a new life. It provided forms of recreation—including gambling—that were forbidden in Utah.

Even so, for many years, West Wendover dwelled in the shadow of its more robust Utah neighbor, but as time passed, the relationship changed. As the air base closed and the military presence ended, increasing numbers of tourists from the Salt Lake City area made the 120-mile trip across the salt flats to test their luck at West Wendover's casinos. By 2000, this flashy town was larger than its older, quieter neighbor across the border.

Another, more isolated border town is Jackpot on Highway 93 near the Idaho state line. Like West Wendover, it came to life as a gambling mecca because casino-style betting was banned on the other side. The town began as a pioneering gaming outpost in the mid-1950s, assumed the name Jackpot in 1959 and claimed a population of more than 1,100 residents in 2010. Twin Falls, Idaho, is 45 miles north.

Shawn Hall, the most diligent historical searcher for data on Elko county's remote rural sites identified nearly 300 ghost towns, stage and railroad stations, forts, mining camps, and similar outposts. His book, *Old Heart of Nevada*, published in 1998, is a monument to his diligence. Most of them are now beyond recognition because of vandalism and the normal decay dictated by the desert climate.

CHAPTER THIRTEEN

Changing Landscapes in the Twentieth Century

When Nevadans experienced a twenty-year period of relative prosperity between 1900 and 1920, the state's upward destiny had apparently resumed. The mining booms at Tonopah, Goldfield, and White Pine County persuaded a new generation of pundits that the state was still rich in mineral resources. The Newlands Project gave a surge of commercial energy to Churchill County, and Clark's railroad suggested that even such a remote outpost as Lincoln County and the oasis at Las Vegas had possibilities. Also, social changes were in the wind.

WOMAN SUFFRAGE SUCCEEDS, PARTIALLY

The most significant change on Nevada's political horizon came in the second decade of the new century, when a rejuvenated woman suffrage movement finally achieved its goal in 1914. After repeated failures in the nineteenth century, it found its main leadership in the historian Anne Martin, who became prominent nationally for her activism. Unlike the suffragists of the previous generation, she was a native daughter, born near Carson City in 1875 and a graduate of the tiny state university in Reno.

After a brief period at Stanford University, she had returned to Reno to teach history and art at her alma mater. Then she traveled to the eastern states and to England in the early 1900s, becoming active in the suffrage movement. Following several years away, she returned again to embrace the cause in Nevada. She organized both men and women across the state as her predecessors had not been able to do.

The Nevada legislature approved a constitutional amendment to extend the vote to women in both 1911 and 1913. (As noted earlier, the State Constitution requires that any proposed amendment must pass legislative muster twice before it can be submitted to the voters.) Martin arrived from her English experience in time to lead the scattered voters of the state to approval during the general election of 1914. She helped organize a grassroots movement to mobilize women across the state, and—more essential—their husbands, brothers, and sons. The suffrage amendment won by a vote of 10,161 to 7,258.

With that victory, Martin seemed to be at the vanguard of a new era. She followed this achievement by two attempts to win election to the U.S Senate in 1918 and 1920. Although both failed, she had the distinction of being one of the first women in the nation to seek such an elevated office. Her biographer, Anne Howard, has paid an appropriate tribute to her legacy.

Yet in the early 1920s, the state seemed to be slipping into another recession after the prosperity that had accompanied World War I. This downturn was not as crippling as the "twenty-year depression" of 1880–1900, but it reminded oldtimers of those dark years.

Many Nevadans sought reasons for the state's economic woes. One of the more thoughtful essays came from Anne Martin, who published an analysis of the state's troubles, written after her second Senate attempt. Her article, titled, "NEVADA: Beautiful Desert of Buried Hopes," appeared in the *Nation* in 1922. She placed most of the blame on livestock barons of the previous generation, whom she accused of strangling the chances of the small farmers.

> The live-stock industry, established as a monopoly in Nevada under very extraordinary conditions, is responsible. It has prevented the development of small farms, of family life, of a stable agricultural population, and has produced an excessive proportion of migratory laborers and homeless men, larger than any state in the Union. The 1910 census figures give 220 men to every 100 women....
>
> Utah has shown our bosses both in Washington and Nevada how to manage large land and water holdings for the public good. It was the policy of the Mormon Church to divide good land into small farms. And Utah, with nearly equal agricultural resources, has a much larger population and greater economic and social stability than her neighbor....

Martin's impassioned analysis was an oversimplification. The problem was not only that the livestock barons had crowded out the small farmers but also the climatic limitations of the region. Nevada's high desert terrain made it almost impossible for family-sized units to prosper in most of the western half of the Great Basin. The growing season was too short, and water for irrigation was much less dependable than in the foothills of Utah's Wasatch Mountains. By the time Martin wrote, hundreds of farmers had tried to transplant the skills learned in the rain-blessed portions of the Mississippi River basin to Nevada—and had failed. The challenges and resources of North-Center were more demanding than those in the Midwest or in Utah. Northern Nevada was suitable for grazing, but not much of it for small farms.

Rangelands: Alfalfa vs. Cheatgrass

Two of the grasses most frequently seen in the rural areas of the North-Center are the much-admired alfalfa and the much-hated cheatgrass. The first is cultivated as a cash crop; the second is dreaded as the destroyer of native flora and the cause of some of the most devastating wildfires of recent times.

Both apparently arrived in the Great Basin as imports from Asia. The respect for alfalfa arises from the fact that it grows readily in many parts of Nevada where irrigation is possible, feeds the livestock, and is a cash crop easily marketed in other states. It is also aesthetically pleasing. As Peter Goin and Paul F. Starrs testified in their 2005 book, *Black Rock,*

> Nothing in the desert is so refreshing, so humanizing, so much a gift as a walk in the early morning or evening past green acres of alfalfa fields, when the coolness from evaporating irrigation water and the puritanically clean smell of blossoming alfalfa come in waves. Some uses of water are essential; growing alfalfa seems a luxury that is emblematic of the delicate hold and the dramatic transformation that desert dwellers have crafted. If alfalfa growing is an enormous indulgence, it is an ancient one; Arabs originated the name for alfalfa and like the farmers of Winnemucca, Lovelock, or Paradise Valley, they irrigated their alfalfa with elaborate waterworks....

It is difficult to find such kind words about that other famous grass, which was apparently also imported from Asia. "Cheatgrass," or "June grass," is widespread in the far West and is now dreaded everywhere as a summer fire hazard. It is one of the first grasses to offer a green carpet to the landscape in the spring and can be a nourishing foodstuff for grazing animals in May, but it becomes a tinderbox in the late summer and fall. Many of the most devastating wildfires of recent years have been attributed to its spread. It has also crowded out numerous native species of nourishing native flora over the past century.

Cheatgrass was first detected and described in research conducted at the University of Nevada between about 1905 and 1910. Some scholars have suggested that it first occurred along the route of the Southern Pacific railroad. Within the next quarter century it became prevalent across much of the West, but definitive proof for the causes of its spread is elusive. The seeds of this and other unwanted plants were apparently distributed in various ways — migrating people, farm machinery that was frequently moved from place to place, seeds that arrived through the mail, and dozens of other intentional and unintentional means. Ironically, cattlemen and sheepherders driving their animals down from the high country early in the last century may have facilitated the spread of cheatgrass by burning the rangelands behind them to eliminate the trees and small shrubbery their animals would not eat. Cheatgrass flourishes in areas that have been recently burned over.

CATTLEMEN VS. SHEEPHERDERS: FEDERAL INTERVENTION AND "SAGEBRUSH REBELLION"

Large operators like Adams–McGill and Sparks–Harrell brought herds of both cattle and sheep on the ranges of the North-Center, but many smaller operators concentrated on producing just one. It was more costly to go into the cattle business than to take a herd of sheep onto the public domain. After the bitter winter of 1889–90, most cattlemen usually decided to raise hay for winter feeding of their animals. Sheep are more effective at browsing the rugged higher terrain of mountain slopes in all kinds of weather. Sheepmen were nomadic, and it was less costly to provide their keep than it was to outfit and maintain a team of cowboys. Basque immigrants and Mormons from Utah and Idaho were the most widely identified of the sheepherders.

Both cowboys and sheepmen had known for decades that the rangelands were being overgrazed—and blamed each other. Because this situation existed in so many states, Congress passed and President Franklin D. Roosevelt signed the Taylor Grazing Act of 1934, which established grazing districts that limited the numbers of animals that could be put on the specific ranges. This program provided for the Bureau of Land Management (BLM) to manage certain government owned land—the most useful of which in Nevada was in the North-Center.

Livestock owners of both kinds had to absorb three severe blows in the early 1930s: (1) when the Great Depression began, it sent market prices for all livestock into a tailspin; (2) the region suffered its most severe drought in twenty years; and (3) the chain of banks operated by George Wingfield (formerly of Winnemucca and Goldfield) crashed, taking with them the money of depositors in his banks in Winnemucca, Elko, and Wells, as well as other parts of the state. Some depositors never recovered their money.

During the half-century between 1925 and 1974, cattlemen had a distinct advantage over the long term. Numbers compiled by the U.S. Census Bureau for those years showed more than 1.1 million head of sheep on the public rangelands in 1925 but only 133,000 in 1974. During the same period, the number of cattle rose from 419,000 head to 633,000. While the cattle population fluctuated during the 1930s, the sheep population declined steadily.

Scholars who have studied these numbers cite several reasons. American consumers had a growing preference for beef, which may be the main explanation. Sheepmen have blamed increased government regulation in the effort to protect the rangeland from overgrazing, restrictions on predator control, and the increased cost of hauling water to their herds.

The year 1976 brought another controversial change in the land-management policy of the federal government—passage by Congress of the Federal Land Policy Management Act (FLPMA). This law added another set of standards for range management and further infuriated livestock owners. Although most scientists believed the added regulations protected the rangelands, local spokesmen became more fervent in their resentment of government regulation.

The next chapter in the Great Basin saga was the "Sagebrush Rebellion," which began in the late 1970s in Elko County. Livestock owners and their allies decided the federal government had gone too far with its regulations. They affirmed that the State of Nevada, not the federal government, should own and manage the public domain. They argued also that the framers of the Nevada Constitution had been improperly forced to renounce the state's proper title to the land when it was admitted to the Union in 1864. When they carried their argument to the Nevada legislature in 1979, their message resulted in an appropriation of $250,000 to pursue litigation in the federal courts.

This idea of state ownership of public lands was a baseless assertion. It yielded no results in the judicial system, but it enlivened political discourse in Nevada for a few years before it faded. The rebels' case was weak, because the state's original constitutional document, approved by voters and by President Lincoln in 1864, had clearly abandoned all state claims to public lands.

The Bureau of Land Management is the federal agency responsible for administering most of this land, which covers more than half of the North Center. It has a broad legal mandate as caretaker of roughly 35 million acres to provide for rangeland management; recreational uses; restoring vast, damaged, overgrazed, and heavily mined areas; protecting places designated as wilderness; and other related responsibilities.

But the Rebellion summarized the extent to which Nevada's rural counties had evolved from the status of dependency, like a child needing help, to a rebellious teenager defying the parent who had nourished it during infancy. Echoes could still be heard in some political circles well into the twenty-first century.

Another federal agency with responsibilities for protecting the natural resources is the U.S. Forest Service. Its jurisdiction is smaller but still consists of well over 5 million acres in Nevada, and its responsibilities are no less important. The Humboldt Toiyabe division of the USFS is the largest in the United States south of Alaska. Most of its acreage is in the high, timbered mountain ranges in the North Center.

CHAPTER FOURTEEN

Spanning the Distances, Part One

Newspapers, Schools, and Churches

PIONEER NEWSPAPERS: THE UNREFINED ORE OF HISTORY

Newspapers appeared in nineteenth-century mining camps like fragile desert flowers after a spring rain. And they usually disappeared as quickly as the changing winds of mining excitement could scatter them. But in the few cases when they survived, they became a crucial source of communication between local readers, the towns, and the broader world.

Soon after prospectors arrived at a promising new place, a printer with his hand-lever press and "shirt-tail-full-of-type" was likely to be close behind. Almost every town with any promise of prosperity, no matter how brief, had its editor, printer, and reporter, often just one or two people. These denizens of the inky trade built a crucial network of information connecting remote outposts with one another. They formed the Internet of the nineteenth century. Sometimes slow to distribute their information, but often more rapid than the sluggish U.S. Mail, their gossip and hyperbole were widely distributed.

Fortunately for historians, hundreds of examples of these early journals have survived. Various publications are available in university libraries, at the Nevada Historical Society, the Bancroft Library of the University of California, and elsewhere. The paper on which they were printed has decayed, but microfilm and electronic resources have preserved many of the texts. Historians Richard E. Lingenfelter and Karen D. Gash assembled a useful bibliography of those founded before 1979. UNLV professor Barbara Cloud condensed much helpful analysis in her 2008 book, *The Coming of the Frontier Press*.

The pages of these early newspapers usually consisted primarily of advertisements (like much electronic and print media of the twenty-first century). They had relatively small space for local or regional information and were invariably "boosters" of their new hometowns. Local gossip was an attraction, as were reports from the mines—both the productive and the potential ones.

Nevada's first newspaper, the *Territorial Enterprise* initially appeared in Genoa in 1858. Its printers moved to Carson City the following year and finally to Virginia City in 1861. It became the most famous periodical in Nevada's early history because of the journalistic high jinks of Mark Twain and Dan DeQuille.

Some of its younger siblings farther east tried to follow the example, but none ever made the grade. Most failed as quickly as the mining towns they were trying to entertain.

A few of these journals survived for many decades, partly because they got contracts with county governments to publish legal notices—court reports, voters' lists, tax information, and other official matters. They also carried information about local political events and the advertisements of area businesses. When a telegraph line arrived in town—the advanced communication technology of the late nineteenth century—the most prosperous of them could regularly bring a taste of national and foreign news to the readers. Later, in the mid-twentieth century, several could claim the advantage of a long-term publisher-editor who had the respect of the readers and could combine his popularity with political privilege.

Elko: Pioneering in Journalism

The *Elko Independent* is our first exhibit. It became available to readers in June 1869, a month after the golden spike closed the gap in the transcontinental railroad at Promontory, Utah. Its printer-publisher had previously invested his talent and type in Unionville but had abandoned that declining mining camp when the railroad was being constructed.

The *Independent* shared its path with Elko, usually as an advocate of Democratic politics, for well over a century. In later years, from 1937 until 1974, it was owned and edited by Warren L. Monroe, one of the state's most respected community leaders. Monroe may serve as an example of those editor-publishers who combined the two functions with political activities. He was elected four times and served sixteen years in the state senate (1959–75). He continued to write a column for several years after he stepped aside as editor.

The *Elko Free Press* became the main rival of the *Independent* after 1882; it was usually pro-Republican. For about ninety years, its business and editorial activities were connected with the family of E. M. Steninger, his son, and grandson. It became a daily in 1931 and managed to sustain that status for three generations. In recent years, it has been absorbed into a national newspaper consortium, although much of the news reporting and opinion is generated locally.

Ely's Newspapers and Its Two Governors

The newspaper history of Ely in the twentieth century merges smoothly into the more extensive history of state politics, for the White Pine copper industry was the prime mover in the recovery of Nevada's mining economy. Ely's newspapers became springboards for two political leaders who ascended to the highest levels of state politics.

When Ely became the county seat of White Pine County in 1887 after the demise of Hamilton, it inherited the *White Pine News*, whose printers had relocated it a couple of times in other camps. It persisted in Ely until the 1920s, when it lost its battle for survival to a competitor, the *Ely Daily Times*, edited by Vail Pittman.

Pittman was a relative newcomer to Ely but his reputation preceded him; he was the younger brother of U.S. Senator Key Pittman. The older Pittman had opened a law practice in Tonopah in 1902 and quickly became the most prominent Democrat in the state, winning election to the U.S. Senate ten years later.

Having established himself in the top ranks of state politics, Senator Key Pittman invited his inexperienced sibling to join him on the frontier. Vail worked various jobs in Tonopah before deciding to relocate in the new copper-producing town to establish the *Ely Daily Times* in 1920. In retrospect, it was a wise decision, because Tonopah's days of prosperity were ending, and those of the Ely's Robinson district were improving.

Vail and his wife Ida managed the *Times* for two decades. Four years after beginning as editor and publisher, Vail was elected to the state senate, which took him to Carson City for the 1925 and 1927 sessions of the legislature. This brief taste of politics whetted his ambition.

Soon after his brother, Key, died in 1940, Vail tried to become the heir to his political mantle. He was elected lieutenant governor in 1942, became acting governor in 1945, and was then elected to a four-year term as governor in 1946. He also became the leading opponent of the political machine of Senator Pat McCarran (whom his brother Key had loathed during the final years of his life).

The magnetic pull of politics took Vail away from Ely and his duties at the *Times*. After his tenure as governor ended in 1950, he sold his Ely paper and moved to Las Vegas.

Vail Pittman's rival in the White Pine newspaper business was Charles Russell, editor and owner of the weekly *Ely Record* from 1929 until 1946. This periodical first appeared as the *Ely Mining Record* at the beginning of the copper-mining era. Russell was a genial Republican who managed to win several terms in the legislature in a county that usually voted heavily Democratic. He served in six sessions from 1935 through 1945, gaining a statewide reputation. Then he ran for Nevada's only seat in the House of Representatives in 1946 and won, the first time in sixteen years a Republican had been chosen for that office. Soon after his election, he sold the *Record* to Pittman.

But the competition was not finished. When Russell lost his bid for a second term in Congress in 1948, he cast his political eye on the governorship. Pittman was seeking re-election to a second term in 1950, and Russell emerged as the preferred standard-bearer on the Republican side. Russell won decisively. Pittman opposed him again in 1954, with the same result. By the time both men retired from politics, their sparring had extended over three decades. In his post-political career Russell settled in Reno. After their time, the path into state political prominence by way of local publishing came to a close.

The *Ely Daily Times* prospered for several more years, but it shared the fate of White Pine County. Its prosperity faded along with the copper industry. By gradual steps, the *Times* reduced its frequency of publication and finally was absorbed into a consortium based in Las Vegas.

Newspaper readers who lived in central and eastern Nevada during the middle years of the twentieth century often got their national and world news from the *Salt Lake Tribune*, which was more readily available than the Reno and Las Vegas papers.

For about twenty years after the 1950s, the few newspapers published in the county seats survived by relying on county government business, local advertising, and the loyalty of subscribers. But since then, increasing numbers of local papers—the "rags" we local readers once enjoyed and ridiculed—have been absorbed into larger chains. Most of the news and entertainment they once provided comes to us in the twenty-first century by electronic media, available on demand.

AUSTIN, EUREKA, PIOCHE, AND WINNEMUCCA

The *Reese River Reveille* helped give Austin its place of honor among the mining camps of central Nevada. It became available to its earliest readers in May 1863, at about the time Austin appeared on the maps of the Territory and became the hub of news and rumor for the North-Center. It had a lifespan of ninety-nine years before being absorbed into a larger cluster of publications based in Tonopah. It faded gently into senility and death, an appropriate emblem of "the town that died laughing."

The *Eureka Sentinel* presented a less colorful narrative than the *Reveille*, but it also enjoyed a long life cycle. Established in 1870 at the beginning of the boom in its hometown, it too was swallowed by the Tonopah group in about 1975. The print shop from which it issued for most of its life became part of Eureka's historic district, a museum with most of its hardware intact.

The *Pioche Record*, also started in 1870, endured for more than 140 years with slightly modified names on the masthead. As Pioche boomed in the 1870s, it quickly evolved from a weekly to a triweekly to a daily, and then reverted to its original weekly schedule. In 1899, at one of the low points in its wobbly history, it suspended publication for four months. When its owner, Herman E. Freudenthal, revived it, he wrote candidly, "Unlike most papers it does not start out with the intention of running first in the interest of the public, but will be run in the interest of the Proprietor and what he can make out of it." Resurrected as a weekly, it managed to survive more or less in the same format for another hundred years. In recent years, it has been known as the *Lincoln County Record*. In 2011, it was absorbed into a newspaper conglomerate published and distributed from Las Vegas.

Winnemucca had an influential newspaper when George Nixon edited the *Silver State* in the 1890s, and his successor, Allen Bragg, stood out briefly as the peripatetic promoter of Humboldt County in 1905. In the next twenty years, management changed hands several times before it finally died in 1925.

A rival was already on the scene, prepared to carry the journalistic torch. The *Humboldt Star* had dared to challenge the *Silver State* as a Republican voice as early as 1906. When the older newspaper folded, the *Star* was ready to absorb its readers and its assets. By then, the *Star* had become the property of Rollin C. Stitser. He or his wife Avery published the *Star* for nearly forty years, until she sold the business to the Donald C. Reynolds conglomerate, which was acquiring newspapers nationwide.

There is no need to continue this sad litany of the life and death of the newspapers of the North Center. The pattern, with slight variations has been similar for many other communities across the nation. Local newspapers, once the most conspicuous public voice of the towns they served, were swallowed into conglomerates and the electronic technology that transformed the world in the late twentieth century.

On another note, radio reception in rural Nevada was an exciting experiment in the 1920s. It improved substantially during the 1930s and 1940s. Long-distance telephoning became more accessible and economical a decade or two later. Widespread television reception became available after mid-century, and fifty years later, the Internet decisively closed the gaps in the flow of news and advertising.

Schools

For the first ninety years, the educational history of the state—especially in the North-Center—was one of struggle by teachers and parents to offer basic skills to children, with modest—even stingy—help from the tax rolls.

Public education was as erratic as journalism in its development on the early Nevada frontier. Like the newspapers that flow-
ered and faded, schools sprang up and often disappeared quickly
in most scattered rural areas until the state government began to
offer help early in the twentieth century.

As of 1900, no statewide system of public education existed.
While an embryonic state university had opened in Reno in 1887
with meager federal and state funding, qualified schoolteachers
were rare, and elementary education was spotty. In Virginia City,
Carson, and Reno, school districts received a pittance of tax money
from the state treasury. In most parts of the North-Center, even
this meager support was not dependable.

The schools that existed were grassroots efforts, started by
parents who wanted their children to learn to read, write, and do
the numbers. A few families would choose a school board, hire
a teacher, and pay her wages for as long as the dollars lasted—
sometimes only three or four months a year. Schoolhouses, where
they existed, were crude cabins, built by the parents. A fortunate
school library might have a donated dictionary, if one was available. Elko County had about sixty school districts in 1900, but
many were not operating.

In the 1890s, Orvis Ring, the articulate State Superintendent
of Public Instruction, traveled throughout the state and put school
improvement near the top of the political agenda. Ring, who was
elected Superintendent four times between 1890 and 1910, became
the conscience of Nevada in educational matters. He used his
biennial reports to the governor and legislature to demonstrate
how derelict Nevada had been in its obligations to prepare young
people for the new century.

Ring worked with Professor Romanzo Adams at the University of Nevada, who directed the teacher-training program. The
two were the architects of a 1907 law that remained in place with
few changes for the next fifty years. It provided more dependable
financial support from the state and arranged for a state board
of education that was empowered to set standards for teachers
and to specify curriculum. This reform movement helped establish
high schools in nearly every county and included vocational and

industrial training. Five newly appointed deputy superintendents were assigned to monitor standards in the hundreds of school districts scattered across the state.

In the fifty years following the 1907 law, the population of the state quadrupled, with most of the increase in Reno and Las Vegas. In the North-Center, some areas added residents during that period, some declined, and the overall change was modest. But the school-age population increased more rapidly as more workers came to the state with families.

By mid-century the need for another major reform was evident. Governor Charles Russell called a special session of the legislature in 1954 to address the problems revealed by the post–World War II population increase. The result was a comprehensive study by Peabody College of Nashville, Tennessee, which condensed some obvious information.

1. Nevada had far too many elementary school districts (nearly 200), but three-fourths were too small to offer adequate educational programs;
2. Nevada had thirty-six high schools, but at least twenty-two were deficient in categories such as vocational training, music, art, and libraries; and
3. The pattern of financing schools was erratic, with some of the richer districts providing good funding but most rural and poorer districts lagging far behind.

Although the Peabody Report did not identify the least effective schools individually, it was clear that many of those in greatest need were in the North-Center. In 1955, the legislature, boldly venturing into a new tax policy, imposed a two-percent sales tax on most retail purchases to support the schools. Soon there was a backlash, but the broad response was a grassroots effort, led by women who called themselves the "Little Mothers," to approve the tax by a referendum in 1956. The reforms of the 1950s also consolidated the dozens of scattered school districts into seventeen, one for each county. They also tried to improve the educational opportunities for students in rural areas through a statewide school distributive fund.

Nevada's public education system—including the rural schools—was gradually improving during the last half of the twentieth century and the first few years of the twenty-first. But the state continued to have a low ranking among the states in its level of financial support for classroom instruction. Between 2007 and 2011, tax support for education fell even further as the Great Recession deepened and the legislature made sharp cuts in state appropriations for schools. Nevada was once again among the lowest of the states when ranked according to the amount of financial support it provided for public education.

A Sampling of Religious and Fraternal Organizations

Newspapers and schools were primary resources that served the social network in the frontier communities. Among others were churches and fraternal orders, where friendships were cultivated and help was available in times of trouble. Before Social Security came to the rescue in the 1930s, these nongovernment groups and clusters of friends were the main safety net for widows, disabled workers, and children in need.

Christian churches followed the prospectors almost as quickly as the newspapers. Three denominations were most prominent in the North-Center towns in the nineteenth century—Catholic, Episcopal, and Methodist. In most areas, the Baptists, Mormons, and evangelical groups came later.

Catholics

Catholic clergymen arrived in Nevada soon after the discovery of the Comstock Lode in 1859. Father Patrick Manogue, a towering Irishman, became the most famous figure in the state annals of the Roman Church because of his charismatic and humane presence, but his influence had a tenuous reach into the North-Center.

Parishes or missions appeared in quick sequence in Austin, Belmont, Hamilton, Cherry Creek, Eureka, and Pioche soon after discoveries of ore. These were seeds for missions and worship stations for a dozen other towns. Much Catholic charitable work flowed from these outposts.

In the early 1880s, when the mining industry foundered in recession, Manogue consolidated his dwindling number of parishes with those in northern California. Within a few years, the western Nevada parishes became part of the diocese of Sacramento.

Meanwhile, Lawrence Scanlon, a priest who had served the Pioche parish in the 1870s, moved to Salt Lake City and became bishop of a diocese that included Utah Territory and most of eastern Nevada. The few parishes that had been established during the prosperous years declined during the "twenty-year depression" and were downgraded to missions or ceased to operate. There was little recovery until thirty years later.

While Irish Catholics were among the most prominent Nevadans of the bonanza years, immigrants from Italy were more conspicuous during the following generation. Many of them had a more relaxed attitude toward the church and its rituals, reflecting the turmoil that was occurring in "the old country" in the late nineteenth century.

In 1931, when the census bureau listed Nevada's population as 91,058, Catholics estimated their membership at 8,500, with only a small number of priests to serve them. Parishes existed at Elko, Ely, Lovelock, and Winnemucca, with missions in a dozen other places in the North-Center.

After another seven decades, with Nevada's population at nearly 2 million, one-fourth of those who were identified with a denomination identified themselves as Catholic.

Latter-day Saints

Mormons were the original pioneers on the Nevada frontier. Their forts at Genoa (1851–57) and Las Vegas (1855–58) marked the first Anglo-American settlements in those regions. Both experiments were short lived, because their leaders recalled them to Salt Lake City during the so-called Utah War. The LDS Church had no organized presence in the North-Center until many decades later, with the exceptions of Panaca and Alamo.

The men who mined the ore and built the railroads often regarded Mormons with contempt and amusement. Up to 1890, when the so-called Woodruff Manifesto announced the end of polygamy, they both criticized and envied the LDS tolerance of the practice. The earliest Nevada historians gave the Mormons only brief attention, presumably because their history was a delicate subject and their numbers were insignificant.

Only a few small wards, (i.e., congregations of Mormon

worshipers) functioned in the scattered towns, most of them in Panaca and other distant villages of southern Lincoln County—the region that became Clark County in 1909. Nearly all these settlers migrated as families.

With two small exceptions, the Latter-day Saints virtually abandoned their efforts to establish communal settlements in the North-Center between the 1850s and the 1920s. These exceptions were at Preston and Lund in the White River Valley of White Pine County, established in 1898. About 15,000 acres of promising grazing land became the property of the Church in 1897 in a business venture. The church created the White Pine Land and Livestock Company, and LDS authorities in Salt Lake City arranged for a bishop from St. George to lead colonies to the region. The two towns were named for southern Utah church authorities.

Most settlers in that area were recruited from Danish and German immigrants who had converted to the Church in their homelands and were attracted to Utah. Church-appointed authorities laid out the towns in the typical grid-manner, organized schools, and established a local court to adjudicate water conflicts. They were slowly absorbed into the White Pine County civil system in the following decades.

In the LDS organizational structure, the next level of administration above the ward is the stake, often consisting of about ten wards. No such unit existed in the state until 1926, when the Nevada Stake was founded, with its base in Ely. Through the 1930s and 1940s, Mormon workers joined the growing labor crews in Elko, Ely, and Pioche.

In 2008, the LDS Church almanac reported that 7.1 percent of the Nevada's population, or nearly 170,000 people, identified as Mormons. It was the second-largest denomination in the state and probably the largest in the North-Center.

Mainline Protestants

Four mainline Protestant churches tried to build congregations in the mining and railroad towns of the North-Center during the 1865–75 boom years. Episcopalians, Methodists, and Presbyterians all sent pioneering ministers to offer their varieties of Christianity to nascent congregations. As usual, they were not far behind prospectors and newspapers in Austin, Hamilton, Eureka, and Pioche. Small congregations continued to exist in the twenty-first century. In a few cases, a church edifice built in earlier times remained as a focal point.

Early Nevada historians recorded the presence of Baptist churches in the Virginia–Carson–Reno area during the bonanza period. Preachers in this religious tradition apparently were not available to follow the migrations to the mining camps and railroad towns as quickly as the Methodists and Episcopalians.

Each mainline Protestant movement has been troubled by schisms in the past 150 years, but Baptists may hold the record for fragmentation. The Civil War produced the most profound of these divisions, and the Southern Baptists emerged from that conflict as the branch that led in numbers and in evangelical missionary efforts. By the 1950s, they were the largest Protestant denomination in the U.S. and the one most committed to missionary work in the far West.

The Southern Baptists initiated a tentative approach to the central Great Basin in the 1940s and organized a surge of missionary activity in Utah, Idaho, and Nevada in the 1950s. They were engaged is active missionary work from bases in Ely and Winnemucca by the mid-1950s and reached out to dozens of isolated towns. In the next quarter century, they had established congregations or missions in at least twenty-five remote places in the North-Center, including Indian Reservations. Often their preachers served only a few families, but they reflected substantial support from the national organization. No other mainline Protestant movement was as evident in more remote spots. As the variety of religious denominations has proliferated across America, Nevada has become fertile ground for their seeds. Most towns have gospel missions or similar stations.

Jews

Jews in Nevada have been few but prominent and influential in politics and business from the earliest years. Their faith tradition has received the most extensive professional examination of all the religious groups in Nevada. John P. Marschall, emeritus professor at the University of Nevada in Reno, has produced a well-researched history of their roles on the Nevada scene (Marschall 2008).

Marcshall's research shows that the small number of Jews who arrived in Nevada in the nineteenth century encountered less anti-Semitic prejudice than their counterparts in more populous areas of the East. In the early years, many Jews were immigrants, and much of Nevada's population was foreign born. There is little record of Jews having faced the intensity of bias that the Italians met, for example, in Eureka during the "charcoal burners" war. Jews became charter members in many fraternal organizations (from which they were often banned in the East). Jewish merchants were usually welcomed in the isolated towns for the services they offered. "Jewish numbers were miniscule compared to the general population," Marschall writes, "but their positions as first arrivals in many Nevada camps and towns assured them of an acceptance unequaled in the Old Country or the nation's eastern cities" (Marschall, xv–xvi).

Marschall's research also turned up several small Jewish communities in rural Nevada in the nineteenth century. In some places, they celebrated traditional holidays, formed benevolent societies, joined fraternal orders, and established burial grounds. As was the case elsewhere, the most vigorous Jewish communities were in the larger cities.

Fraternal Orders

Early Nevadans often found their friendships in groups known as fraternal orders, especially Masons and Odd Fellows. Most mining and railroad towns built halls where members could meet for companionship and offer assistance before local governments there had the resources to reach out. They were so-called "secret orders," presumably because they had passwords and rituals known only to members. The "secrecy" was a legacy of earlier times when such groups were officially banned by governments in Europe, who were afraid of their revolutionary possibilities. By the nineteenth century, such groups maintained confidentiality because they did not want to spread rumors about the charitable work they were doing. The Masons and Odd Fellow lodges built substantial meeting halls in several towns, which became alternatives to the saloons and the houses of ill fame. In my most recent visits to some of the towns in the North Center, several Masonic or Odd Fellows halls were visible, mute reminders of the humanitarian and social services they provided before the governments were ready to help. Most often they have been replaced or transformed into more commercial purposes.

CHAPTER FIFTEEN

Spanning the Distances, Part Two

Connecting the North-Center to the Nation

Roads and Highways

As the twentieth century began, the trails between towns and ranches were hardened by the hooves of animals and the wheels of the wagons they often pulled. In some years, the trails were ruts of snow or mud from autumn to spring. The various governments—county, state, and federal—had little money for roads before the automobile bumped its way onto the landscape in the early 1900s.

When the horseless carriages became more common, Nevada's legislature first tried to build roads by using inmate labor from the state prison. The experiment was an expensive failure; prisoners did not do good work and too often walked away. The lawmakers finally decided it was necessary to register the new-fangled automobiles for a fee and tax the gasoline they used.

A nudge from the federal government boosted Nevada into the road-building business. In 1916, when the auto was still a novelty but becoming more common, Congress passed a law encouraging the states to establish highway departments and offering to pay half the cost of improving postal roads. This was the modest but crucial beginning of a national highway policy. The Nevada legislature jumped on board the following year by appropriating funds for a state highway engineer. But neither the counties nor the state had adequate money for substantial improvements.

Federal dollars arrived in a slow trickle during the 1920s. U.S. Senator Tasker L. Oddie (the same man who began his Nevada career in Austin and started his political climb in Tonopah) had bounced and bumped his way between the towns and ranches in an automobile. During his two terms in the Senate (1921–33) he made road building with federal government funding his highest priority. The culmination of his efforts was the Oddie–Colton Public Domain Highway Act, signed into law by President Herbert Hoover in 1930. It offered federal financial support for highway construction, based on the amount of land owned by the U.S. government within the boundaries of each state. Since federal ownership in Nevada was nearly ninety percent, it was a windfall for the state, especially the North-Center.

This formula brought millions of dollars flowing into Nevada for road building during the 1930s and for the next eighty years. East-west highways 40 and 50, and north-south highways 93 and 95, which connect most towns within the state, were built mostly with federal funds.

When Interstate 80 — now called Eisenhower Freeway — replaced U.S. 40 in the 1960s as the primary route along the Humboldt trail, it reshaped the economic lives of the old Central Pacific towns. Highway 40 threaded its way through the centers of the historic communities built around the railroad. Hardware stores, gas stations, grocery stores, small restaurants, and saloons had offered their rustic services to local clients and travelers for decades. The small motels, spaced along the main drag, were a post–World War II innovation.

But after the freeway bypassed the main streets of Lovelock, Winnemucca, Battle Mountain, Elko, and Wells, most of those businesses withered or were replaced. The new interstate offered access to the towns by on-off ramps, where the newer business establishments appeared, often at the expense of the older "downtown" clusters. The newer, post-freeway places simply had faster and more convenient access to I-80. New accommodations were usually more luxurious and managed by national chains. The local innkeepers were hard pressed to compete when the national corporations arrived. These changes accelerated the process of making Nevada's commercial centers more like those elsewhere across the nation.

Telephone, Television, and Internet

The history of telephone service follows a similar pattern of consolidation. Small, locally managed exchanges gradually emerged as the result of dozens of private investments. In the earliest experiments with Alexander Graham Bell's new toy in about 1900, two or three families hooked their houses together along barbed-wire fence lines. As the technology evolved, the local phone systems emerged—with wires stretched between several houses or offices. By the 1950s, it was possible to make a long-distance call from Reno to eastern Nevada, if one had enough patience and a pocketful of coins to pay for operators to link her through Salt Lake City to the place she wanted in the distant North-Center. A call from Reno to Pioche, for example, might require a half hour at a public pay phone in a restaurant, waiting for connecting lines to be opened by a network of intermediate operators. The twenty-first century wireless and Internet connections among Nevadans and the wider world, now taken for granted by younger generations, are still a mystery to some oldtimers. Within a single lifetime, we have been absorbed into the international economy and culture(s) in ways that our grandparents could not have imagined.

Nevada's main employers of the first seventy-five years of our survey were mining, agriculture, and railroads. In the most recent seventy-five years, gaming, tourism, and all levels of government are often more prominent. As mining has provided the most obvious success story in recent years for the North-Center, let us take that as our final metaphor. The long-time observer will question its durability. How long can it continue and what refuse and problems will it leave behind after the excavators and refiners have gone? The historical record does not provide much reason for optimism.

Through six generations, thousands of itinerant prospectors have searched for their bonanzas. Many, like Sam Clemens in Unionville, believed they had found it only to be soon disappointed. Very few were able to confirm their hunches and realize their treasure. When, on rare occasions, they have hit pay dirt, it has usually been the middlemen, the promoters, the brokers, the international investors who saw the big profits from discovery and development.

The quest for rocks that could be pummeled and processed to produce precious metal can become a kind of addiction. From the forty-niners who rushed across this inland terrain in search of California gold to the international corporations of the late twentieth and twenty-first centuries, the passion was similar.

Federal Agencies: Connectors and Neighbors

The two U.S. government agencies that arouse special interest in the North-Center in the twenty-first century are the Bureau of Land Management and the U.S. Forest Service. They administer more than eighty percent of the region.

The BLM, a unit within the Department of Interior, has a wide range of responsibilities over the vast area it administers—more than half of the North-Center. Its mission is to conserve publicly owned resources and make them available for responsible use. Among other duties, it is mandated to prevent and fight wildfires; manage the rangelands; control wild horse populations; maintain campgrounds and hiking trails; and administer oil and gas leases. It gets mixed reviews from some special interests groups that seek more privileges for private users, but its services are widely admired by conservationists. And in recent years its image has improved, perhaps because it has taken more care to listen to local concerns.

The companion agency, the U.S. Forest Service, has a smaller area to manage but is custodian of some of the wooded uplands. The Humboldt–Toiyabe National Forest—ninety percent of which is in Nevada—is the largest national forest in the lower forty-eight states. The Forest Service protects forests, administers campgrounds, trailheads, and hundreds of miles of paths and several wilderness areas—most of them in the North-Center.

Students of Western American history often return to the time-worn Turner Thesis, a landmark of American historiography. In 1893, Professor Frederick Jackson Turner, of the University of Wisconsin and later Harvard, proposed that the idea of a frontier had inspired the American people from the beginning of their history. As of 1890, Turner argued, that era ended because the distinct frontier line could not be identified any longer between those areas that had two residents per square mile and those that did not. He was mostly right, and as the decades passed, his thesis became more appropriate.

Many contemporary historians who have addressed the subject have found it necessary to dissent or modify the thesis. But in parts of the interior West, Turner's Frontier Thesis has had an

afterglow: most of the North-Center and the bordering regions of southeastern Oregon, southern Idaho, and western Utah still qualified in 2015. The small Nevada cities and towns mentioned here are examples. The vast mountains and valleys are exceptions to his thesis that the frontier closed 125 years ago. Modern media and transportation have not completely conquered the distances.

Reprise, 2016

To the casual traveler rushing across the Great Basin in 2016, the landscape looks much as it did 150 years ago. Electrical power lines and road signs are here now, plus the industrial islands and occasional huge waste dumps. But mostly the landscape between the towns is the same as what the earliest pioneers saw.

When we glance back at the communities along both Highway 50 and I-80, we find these places seem especially eager to celebrate and cling to their early histories. Fallon, in the middle of second decade of the twenty-first century is the most vibrant of these on Highway 50. Its wooden courthouse and the former Oaks schoolhouse—both a century old—are special objects of pride.

Austin, with only a two or three hundred residents remaining, probably has more long-distance supporters than can be found on its streets. Its infrastructure is gradually decaying, but newer homes and businesses are sprouting in the adjacent Reese River Valley.

Eureka's good fortune with a quarter-century gold boom enabled its county government to restore and expand a dozen public buildings. As metal prices fell after 2011, it still had a cushion to reduce the shock.

Ely is the tenacious renaissance city, celebrating its past with its Renaissance Village, calling attention to the region's ethnic diversity. Its early mining history and museum are emphasized as attractions. And mining in a modified form survives as a leading industry.

The Lincoln County towns on U.S. Highway 93—Pioche, Panaca, Caliente, and Alamo—have not yet found their renaissance. Mining and railroading vitality are fading memories. Highway 93 does not stimulate the level of traffic that is found further north.

The half-dozen cities and towns on Interstate 80 appeared more robust in the second decade of the twenty-first century. The commercial stimulus of the freeway, the continuing railroad service, and the gold mining of recent decades have enabled them to remain healthy, and in some cases to grow in population.

Lovelock is the least changed of these I-80 communities, perhaps because it is less directly affected by the gold fever, and thus its success in highlighting its past is more modest.

Investors in Winnemucca and Elko have tried to replicate on a smaller scale the "Nevada-style entertainment" of Las Vegas and Reno with a sequence of casinos and entertainment venues. Battle Mountain, apparently the least economically vigorous of this group, has opted to make a new departure with its innovative courthouse. But to the casual observer looking back fifty years or so, the glittering casinos seem to come and go like the mining camps of the past, though perhaps not as rapidly.

This book has tried to emphasize several subcultures in the *other* Nevada. Railroad builders and homesteaders have shared the terrain. Mining men and Mormons have lived side by side. Cattlemen and sheepherders have contested for the same terrain but have a lesser role these days; grubstakers, prospectors, and gamblers have washed across the Basin with impunity and, like locusts, have often moved on.

There are no skyscrapers out there; it would be a challenge to find any buildings taller than Hotel Nevada in Ely—six stories. Power grids we take for granted, but they are minute in their contexts. A traffic problem would be an obscenity, probably caused by road repairs or an accident.

The most obvious fact about these towns is the space surrounding and between them.

Changing Demographics, 1900–2010

The North-Center includes about two-thirds of Nevada's land, divided into eight or nine counties. Less than five percent of the state's population resides here.

COUNTY	AREA SQUARE MILES (SINCE 1920)	POPULATION		
		1900	1950	2010
Churchill	5,024	830	6,161	24,877
Elko	17,203	5,688	11,654	48,818
Eureka	4,180	1,954	896	1,987
Humboldt	9,658	4,463	4,838	16,528
Lander	5,519	1,534	1,850	5,775
Lincoln	10,637	3,284*	3,837	5,345
Nye (Northern)	3,000?	?	?	?
Pershing	6,067	#	3,103	6,753
White Pine	8,894	1,961	9,424	10,030
Totals	ca. 70,000	19,714	41,763	ca. 120,000

* Before 1909, Lincoln County included all of Clark County.
# Before 1919, Pershing County was part of Humboldt County.

The largest population increases have occurred along the old Humboldt Trail—the route of the first continental railroad of 1868 and the Eisenhower Freeway of the 1960s. This is also the zone where most gold mining and processing has occurred in the last forty years. Additional growth is evident in Churchill County, where several federal projects have stimulated the local economy.

Bibliography

Albrandt, Keith Alan. "Twentieth-Century Copper Mining in White Pine County, Nevada." Master's thesis, University of San Diego, 2008.

Allen, George J. and Gamin Summers. *McGill: The Man, the Town, the Bar.* 48HourBooks, 2014.

Ambrose, Stephen E. *Nothing Like It in the World: The Men Who Built the Transcontinental Railroad, 1863–1869.* New York: Simon & Shuster, 2000.

Anderson, Jim. *Lost in Austin: A Nevada Memoir.* Reno: University of Nevada Press, 2009.

Andrew, Patricia. "Fallon: The Oasis of Nevada." PhD diss., University of Nevada, Reno, 1998.

Angel, Myron, ed. *Thompson & West's History of Nevada, 1881, with illustrations and biographical sketches of its prominent men and pioneers.* Introduction by David Myrick. Reprint, Berkeley: Howell-North, 1958.

Arrington, Leonard J. The *Mormons in Nevada.* Las Vegas: Las Vegas Sun, 1979.

——. *Great Basin Kingdom: An Economic History of the Latter-day Saints, 1830–1900.* Cambridge: Harvard University Press, 1958.

Bragg, Allen C. *Humboldt County: 1905.* Winnemucca: North Central Nevada Historical Society, 1976.

Brooks, Juanita. "A Place of Refuge." *Nevada Historical Society Quarterly* 14, no. 1 (1971) 13–24.

Buck, Franklin A. *A Yankee Trader in the Gold Rush: The Letters of Franklin A. Buck.* Boston: Houghton Mifflin, 1930.

Callaghan, Eugene. *Geology of the Delamar District: Lincoln County, Nevada.* Reno: University of Nevada Bulletin, Mackay School of Mines 31, no. 5, December 1937.

Carlson, Helen. *Nevada Place Names: A Geographical Dictionary.* Reno: University of Nevada Press, 1974.

Chan, Loren. *Sagebrush Statesman: Tasker L. Oddie of Nevada.* Reno: University of Nevada Press, 1973.

Church of Jesus Christ of Latter-day Saints. *2008 Church Almanac.* Salt Lake City: Deseret Morning News, 2008.

Cline, Gloria Griffen. *Exploring the Great Basin*. Norman: University of Oklahoma Press, 1963.

———. *Peter Skene Ogden and the Hudson's Bay Company*. Norman: University of Oklahoma Press, 1974.

Cloud, Barbara. *The Coming of the Frontier Press: How the West Was Really Won*. Foreword by Alan K. Simpson. Evanston, IL: Northwestern University Press, 2008.

Couch, Bertrand F. and Jay A. Carpenter. *Nevada's Metal and Mineral Production (1859–1940, inclusive)*. Reno: Nevada State Bureau of Mines, 1943.

Curran. Harold. *Fearful Crossing: The Central Overland Trail Through Nevada*. Great Basin Press, 1982.

Dahl, Albin B. *Nevada's Economic Development: An Overview*. Reno: UNR Bureau of Business Research, 1977.

Daily Territorial Enterprise. 6 January 1871, 3:2; 12 August 1871; 2:1.

Dalin, David D. and Charles A. Fracchia. "Forgotten Financier: Francois L.A. Pioche," *California Historical Quarterly* 53, no. 1 (1974) 17–24.

Davis, Kenneth S. *FDR: The New Deal Years, 1933–1937*. New York: Random House, 1986.

Davis, Sam P., ed. *The History of Nevada*. Illustrated. Reno: Elms Publishing, 1913. 2 vols.

Di Certo, Joseph J. *The Saga of the Pony Express*. Missoula, MT: Mountain Press, 2002.

Doten, Samuel Bradford. *An Illustrated History of the University of Nevada*. Reno: University of Nevada, 1924.

Earl, Philip I. "Bustles, Broadsides and Ballots: The Story of the Woman Suffrage Movement in Northeastern Nevada, 1869–1914," *Northeastern Nevada Historical Society Quarterly*, Spring, Summer, Fall, 1976.

———. "A Monument More Enduring than Bronze: The Woman Suffrage Movement in North Central Nevada." *The Humboldt Historian*, Winter-Spring 4 (1981): 3–42.

Elliott, Russell R. *Growing Up in a Company Town: A Family in the Copper Camp of McGill, Nevada*. Reno: Nevada Historical Society, 1990.

———.*History of Nevada* (with the assistance of William D. Rowley). 2nd ed. Lincoln: University of Nebraska Press, 1987.

———. *Nevada's Twentieth-Century Mining Boom: Tonopah, Goldfield, Ely*. Reno: University of Nevada Press, 1966.

Fisher, Marion S. Papers, 1955–73. University of Nevada, Reno, Special Collections.

Forbes, Jack D., ed. *Nevada Indians Speak*. Reno: University of Nevada Press, 1967.

Ford, Jean and James W. Hulse. "The First Battle for Woman Suffrage in

Nevada, 1869–1871: Correcting and Expanding the Record." *Nevada Historical Society Quarterly* 38, no. 3 (1995): 174–88.

Fox, William L. *Mapping the Empty: Eight Artists and Nevada*. Foreword by Jeff Kelley. Reno: University of Nevada Press, 1999.

Friends of the Northern Nevada Railroad Committee. *Northern Nevada Railway and the Copper Camps of White Pine County, Nevada*. Ely: 1991.

Gallagher, Morris F. et. al. *History of the Northeastern Nevada Historical Society: The First 50 Years*. Elko: Northeastern Nevada Historical Society Quarterly, no. 1., 2006.

George Peabody College for Teachers. *Public Education in Nevada: Survey Report*. Nashville, TN: 1954.

Georgetta, Clel. *Golden Fleece in Nevada*. Reno: Venture Publishing, 1972.

Gilbert, Bil. *Westering Man: The Life of Joseph Walker*. New York: Atheneum, 1983.

Glass, Mary Ellen. *Silver and Politics in Nevada: 1892–1902*. Reno: University of Nevada Press, 1969.

Glass, Mary Ellen and Al Glass. *Touring Nevada: A Scenic and Historic Guide*. Reno: University of Nevada Press, 1983.

Glotfelty, Cheryll, ed., *Literary Nevada: Writings from the Silver State*. Reno: University of Nevada Press, 2008.

Goin, Peter and Paul F. Starrs. *Black Rock*. Reno: University of Nevada Press, 2005.

Gold Hill Daily News. 7 June 1865, 2:3.

Graham, Andrea. *White Pine County: Where the Great Basin Highway Meets the Loneliest Road in America*. Carson City: Nevada Arts Council, 2003.

Grayson, Donald K. *The Desert's Past: A Natural Prehistory of the Great Basin*. Washington, D.C.: Smithsonian Institution Press, 1993.

Green, Michael S. *Nevada: A History of the Silver State*. Reno: University of Nevada Press, 2015.

Greenhaw, Charles. *Memoirs of Great Basin College* Elko: n.d. Manuscript on file, Great Basin College Library, Elko NV.

——. "Wall Street West: Action in West Wendover," in *East of Eden: West of Zion: Essays on Nevada*, Wilbur S. Shepperson, ed. Reno, Las Vegas: University of Nevada Press, 1989.

Hall, Shawn. *Old Heart of Nevada: Ghost Towns and Mining Camps of Elko County*. Reno, Las Vegas: University of Nevada Press, 1998.

Hall, Stephen L. "Utah in Nevada: Expected and Aberrant Landscapes in the Village of Panaca, Nevada." Master's thesis, University of Nevada, Reno, 2004.

Hardesty, Donald L. *Mining Archaeology in the American West: A View from the Silver State*. Lincoln: University of Nebraska Press, 2010.

Hickson, Howard. *Elko, Nevada: One of the Last Frontiers of the American West*. Elko: Northeastern Nevada Museum, 2002.

Hokanson, Drake. *The Lincoln Highway: Main Street across America*. Iowa City: University of Iowa Press, 1988.

Holderman, Orville. "Jewett W. Adams and W.N. McGill: Their Lives and Ranching Empire." Master's thesis, University of Nevada, Reno, 1963.

Hopkins, Sarah Winnemucca. *Life Among the Paiutes: Their Wrongs and Claims*. New York: G.P. Putnam's Sons, 1883. Reissue, with new foreword by Catherine S. Fowler, Reno: University of Nevada Press, 1994.

Howard, Anne Bail. *The Long Campaign: A Biography of Anne Martin*. Reno: University of Nevada Press, 1985.

Hulse, James W. "The Afterlife of St. Mary's County; or, Utah's Penumbra in Eastern Nevada." *Utah Historical Quarterly* 55, no. 3 (1987): 236–249.

——. *Forty Years in the Wilderness: Impressions of Nevada, 1940–1980*. Reno: University of Nevada Press, 1986.

——. *Lincoln County Nevada: The History of a Mining Region*, Reno: University of Nevada Press, 1971.

——. *The University of Nevada: A Centennial History*. Reno: University of Nevada Press, 1974.

——. *Nevada's Environmental Legacy*. Reno: University of Nevada Press, 2009.

Hunke, Edmund William, Jr. *Southern Baptists in the Intermountain West, 1940–1989: A Fifty-Year History of Utah, Idaho*. Franklin, TN: Providence House, 1998.

Hyslop, Larry. *Sagebrush Heart: Sagebrush Landscape of Elko County, Nevada*. Elko: Gray Jay Press, 2009.

Jackson, W. Turrentine. *Treasure Hill: Portrait of a Silver Mining Camp*. Tucson: University of Arizona Press, 1963.

——. *Wagon Roads West. A Study of Federal Road Surveys and Construction in the Trans-Mississippi West, 1846–1869*. New Haven: Yale University Press, 1965.

James, Ronald M. *Temples of Justice: County Courthouses of Nevada*. Foreword by Cliff Young. Reno, Las Vegas: University of Nevada Press, 1994.

James, Ronald M. and Elizabeth Stafford Harvey. *Nevada's Historic Buildings: A Cultural Legacy*. Photographs by Thomas Perkins. Reno: University of Nevada Press, 2009.

Katzer, Terry and David J. Donovan. *Surface-water Resources and Basin Water Budget for Spring Valley, White Pine and Lincoln Counties, Nevada*, for the Las Vegas Valley Water District. Las Vegas: 2003.

King, Buster L. "The History of Lander County." Master's thesis, University of Nevada, Reno, 1954.

Kolvet, Renee Corona and Victoria Ford. *The Civilian Conservation Corps in Nevada*. Reno: University of Nevada Press, 2006.

Lambert, Darwin. *Great Basin Drama: The Story of a National Park*. Niwot, CO: Roberts Rinehart, 1991.

Larson, Andrew Karl. *"I Was Called to Dixie," the Virgin River Basin: Unique Experiences in Mormon Pioneering*. Salt Lake City: Deseret News Press, 1961.

Las Vegas Valley Water District. *Environmental Report Covering Selected Hydrographic Basins in Clark, Lincoln, Nye and White Pine Counties, Nevada*. Cooperative Water Project 14, 1994.

———. *Water Resources and Ground-Water Modeling in the White River and Meadow Valley Flow Systems: Clark, Lincoln, Nye and White Pine Counties, Nevada*. Las Vegas: 2001.

Laxalt, Robert. "The Other Nevada," *National Geographic* 145 (1974): 733–60.

Lewis, Oscar. *The Town That Died Laughing: The Story of Austin, Nevada, Rambunctious Early-Day Mining Camp, and of Its Renowned Newspaper, the Reese River Reveille*. Boston: Little Brown, 1955. Reprint, Reno: University of Nevada Press, 1986.

Lillard, Richard G. *Desert Challenge: An Interpretation of Nevada*. New York: Alfred A. Knopf, 1942.

Lingenfelter, Richard E. and Karen Rix Gash. *The Newspapers of Nevada: A History and Bibliography, 1854–1979*. Reno: University of Nevada Press, 1984.

Long, Walter S. *Brushwork Diary: Watercolors of Early Nevada*. Text by Michael J. Brodhead and James C. McCormick. Reno: University of Nevada Press, 1991.

Lucier, Gary S. "The Economic Impacts of Introducing Sheep To Range Cattle Operations in Northeastern Nevada." Master's thesis, University of Nevada, Reno, 1980.

Mackedon, Michon. *BOMBAST: Spinning Atoms in the Desert*. Reno: Black Rock Institute Press, 2010.

Madsen, Brigham D. *Glory Hunter: A Biography of Patrick Edward Connor*. Salt Lake City: University of Utah Press, 1990.

Marschall, John P. *Jews in Nevada: A History*. Reno: University of Nevada Press, 2008.

Martin, Anne. "Nevada: Beautiful Desert of Buried Hopes," *Nation* 115 (26 July 1922): 89–92.

———. "The Story of the Nevada Equal Suffrage Campaign: Memoir of Anne Martin," edited with introduction and notes by Austin E. Hutcheson. Reno: *University of Nevada Bulletin* 42:7 (1948): 3–19.

McDonald, Russell W. "Early Courthouses and Lawyers of Humboldt County," *The Humboldt Historian* 1:1 (1974): 2–8.

McKinney, Matthew and William Harmon. *The Western Confluence: A Guide to Governing Natural Resources*. Washington, D.C.: Island Press, 2004.

McPhee, John. *Basin and Range*. New York: Farrar, Straus & Giroux, 1981.

Molinelli, Lambert. *Eureka and Its Resources. A Complete History of Eureka County, Nevada*. San Francisco: H. Keller, 1879. Reprint, Reno: University of Nevada Press, 1982.

Moody, Eric N. "The Early Years of Casino Gambling in Nevada: 1931–1945." PhD diss., University of Nevada, Reno, 1997.

———. "Nevada's Legalization of Casino Gambling in 1931: Purely a Business Proposition." *Nevada Historical Society Quarterly* 37:2 (1994): 79–100.

Moore, Roberta and Scott Slovic, eds. *Wild Nevada: Testimonies on Behalf of the Desert*. Reno: University of Nevada Press, 2005.

Morgan, Dale. *The Humboldt: Highroad of the West*. Rivers of America Series. New York: Farrar & Rinehart, 1943.

Muir, John. *Steep Trails: California, Utah, Nevada, Oregon, The Grand Cañon*. Boston: Houghton Mifflin, 1918.

Myrick, David F. *Railroads of Nevada and Eastern California*. Vol. 1, *The Northern Roads*. Berkeley: Howell North, 1962.

Nevada. Division of Environmental Protection. *Quality of the Environment Report*. Carson City: Division of Environmental Protection, 2001.

———. *Inaugural Message of Gov. James G. Scrugham to the Legislature of 1923*. Thirty-First Session. Carson City: State Printing Office, 1923.

———. *Political History of Nevada*. Issued by Secretary of State Dean Heller. Carson City: State Printing Office, 2006.

Nevada Telecommunications Association. *Fencepost to Fiber: Histories of the Telephone Industry in Nevada, 1887–1997*. Nevada Telecommunications Association, 1998.

Paher, Stanley W. *Nevada Ghost Towns and Mining Camps*. Las Vegas: Nevada Publications, 1970.

Patera, Alan H. *Belmont, Nevada*. Lake Grove, OR: Western Places, 2005.

Patterson, Edna B., Louise A. Ulph, and Victor Goodwin. *Nevada's Northeastern Frontier*. Reno: University of Nevada Press, 1991.

Patterson, Edna. *This Land Was Ours: An In-depth Study of a Frontier Community*. Springville, UT: Art City Publishing, 1973.

Rafferty, Kevin. "Catholics in Nevada," in *Community in the American West*, ed. Stephen Tchudi. Reno: Nevada Humanities Committee, 1999.

Rathbun, Daniel C.B. *Nevada Military Place Names of the Indian Wars and Civil War*. Las Cruces, NM: Yucca Tree Press, 2002.

Raymond, C. Elizabeth. *George Wingfield: Owner and Operator of Nevada*. Reno: University of Nevada Press, 1992.

Reeve, W. Paul. *Making Space on the Western Frontier: Mormons, Miners, and Southern Paiutes*. Urbana: University of Illinois Press, 2006.

Reichman, Frederick Wallace. "Early History of Eureka County, Nevada, 1863–1890." Master's thesis, University of Nevada, Reno, 1967.

Ronald, Ann and Stephen Trimble. *Earthtones: A Nevada Album*. Reno: University of Nevada Press, 1995.

Rowley, William T. *Reclaiming the Arid West: The Career of Francis G. New-lands*. Bloomington: Indiana University Press, 1996.

Sawyer, Grant. *Hang Tough: Grant Sawyer, an Activist in the Governor's Mansion*. Reno: University of Nevada Oral History Program, 1993.

Schyler, Krista. *Gambling on the Water Table: The High-Stakes Implications of the Las Vegas Pipeline For Plants, Animals, Places, and People*. Washington, D.C.: Defenders of Wildlife, 2007.

Schneider, Carolyn. *Bing: On the Road to Elko*. Las Vegas: Stephens Press, 2009.

Shepperson, Wilbur S. *Mirage-Land: Images of Nevada*. With Ann Harvey. Foreword by Ann Ronald. Reno: University of Nevada Press, 1984.

———. *Restless Strangers: Nevada's Immigrants and Their Interpreters*. Reno: University of Nevada Press, 1970.

Simpson, James H. *Survey. Report of Explorations Across the Great Basin of the Territory of Utah For a Direct Wagon-Route from Camp Floyd to Genoa, in the Carson Valley, in 1859*. Washington, D.C.: Government Printing Office, 1876.

Starrs, Paul Francis. "Home Ranch: Ranchers, the Federal Government, and the Partitioning of of Western North American Rangeland." PhD diss., University of California, Berkeley, 1989.

Stegner, Wallace E. *Mormon Country*. New York: Duell, Sloan and Pearce, 1942.

Townley, John M. *Alfalfa Country: Nevada Land, Water, and Politics in the 19th Century*. Reno: University of Nevada Agricultural Experiment Station, 1981.

———. *Conquered Provinces: Nevada Moves Southeast, 1864–1871*. Charles Redd Monographs in Western History. Provo, UT: Brigham Young University Press, 1973.

———. *The Overland Stage: A History and Guidebook*. Reno: Jamison Station Press, 1994.

———. *Turn This Water Into Gold: The Story of the Newlands Project*. 2nd ed. Edited and additional chapters by Susan A. James. Reno: Nevada Historical Society, 1998.

Trimble, Stephen. *The Sagebrush Ocean: A Natural History of the Great Basin*. Reno: University of Nevada Press, 1989.

Twain, Mark. *Roughing It [1872]*. Mark Twain Library, Book 8, 3rd revised edition. Berkeley: University of California Press, 2011.

University of Nevada Cooperative Extension. "2008-2009 Pershing County Agricultural Statistics," by Steve Foster. Fact Sheet 10-12. Reno: 2010.

U.S. Bureau of Land Management. *Clark, Lincoln, and White Pine Counties Groundwater Development Project Final Environmental Impact Statement, 2800 (NV910)*. Reno: Bureau of Land Management Nevada State Office, 2012.

U.S. *Census Report. Vol. 1 Twelfth Census of the United States. Taken in the year 1900. Population.* Part 1. Washington, D.C.: United States Census Office, 1901: 264–65.

U.S. Department of Commerce. *Census of Population: 1950.* Vol. 1. *Number of Inhabitants.* Washington, D.C.: Government Printing Office, 1952: 264–65.

U.S. Department of the Interior. *Compendium of the Tenth Census (June 1, 1880).* Washington, D.C.: Government Printing Office, 1883.

Wall Street Journal, 9 April 2009. "Jobless Rush to Nevada Town's Gold-Plated Economy," A4.

Watson, Anita Ernst. *Into Their Own: Nevada Women Emerging into Public Life.* Reno: Nevada Humanities Committee, 2000.

Wheat, Margaret M. *Survival Arts of the Primitve Paiutes.* Reno: University of Nevada Press, 1967.

White, Richard. *Railroaded: The Transcontinentals and the Making of Modern America.* New York: Norton, 2011.

Wines, Claudia. *Elko County.* Charleston, SC: Acadia, 2008.

——. "Nevada Governors with Ties to Northeastern Nevada," *Northeastern Nevada Historical Society Quarterly.* Elko: 2003–04.

Young, James A. and B. Abbott Sparks. *Cattle in the Cold Desert.* Expanded edition. Reno: University of Nevada Press, 2002.

Young, James A. and Charles D. Clements. *Cheatgrass: Fire and Forage on the Range.* Reno: University of Nevada Press, 2009.

Zanjani, Sally. *A Mine of Her Own: Women Prospectors in the American West, 1850–1950.* Lincoln: University of Nebraska Press, 1997.

——. *Sarah Winnemucca.* Lincoln: University of Nebraska Press, 2001.

About the Author

During his thirty-five year career as Professor of History at the University of Nevada, Reno, Jim Hulse taught European and Russian history courses, drawing on his research at Stanford University, where he earned a Ph.D. This was the primary focus of his early career. Two of his books were published by Stanford University Press and Oxford University Press. In later career, he has focused on Nevada.

Hulse has published often with the University of Nevada Press, including two textbooks and others on subjects as diverse as university history, the state's environment, libraries, and politics. His affection for the rural areas has drawn him back to his home turf.

Index

Page numbers in *italics* indicate illustrations.
The letter "t" after a page number indicates table data.

Adams, Jewett W., 60–61
Adams, Romanzo, 137
African–Americans, 51, 56
agriculture: in Big Meadows, 110; challenges and opportunities, 50, 59, 62–63, 126–27; cheatgrass spread through, 128; in Churchill County, 68, 69–70; experiments, 71; instruction in, 31; land for, 33, 58; military establishment impact on, 69–70; in Pahranagat Valley, 101; in Pershing County, 110, 113; water management and, 67; in Winnemucca, 112–13
air bases, 104, 123, 124
Alamo (town), 102, 149
Alamo ranch, 60
alfalfa, 50, 62, 66, 67, 110, 113, 127
Ambrose, Stephen, 26
Anderson, Jim, 24–25
Anglo–Americans, 26
Argenta Mountains, 28. *See also* Battle Mountain
Arizona Territory, 38
Art Deco, 99
Artemisia tridentada, 5
Ashley, Dole: state line move, participation in, 37

Atomic Energy Commission (AEC), 71, 72
Austin: Battle Mountain compared to, 113; current conditions, 149; newspapers, 135; Pioche compared to, 42; Territorial period, 22–25; towns linked to, 28–29
automobiles, 88, 116, 145

"back-haul rate," 32
Baker, 96
Bancroft Library, 131
Baptists, 139, 142
Barrick Goldstrike Mine, *81*
Battle Mountain: Central Pacific Railroad (CPRR) impact on, 32; courthouse, 114, 150; current conditions, 150; population, 109; prospects, 113–14; railroad station established at, 28–29
Bell, Alexander Graham, 147
Belmont, 35–36, 42
Belmont District, 35
big game collections, 113, 121
Big Meadows, 27, 55, 62, 109–10
Black Rock (Goin and Starrs), 127
Black Rock Desert, 5, 116
Blasdel, Henry G., 38

Bombast (Mackedon), 72
Bonneville Salt Flats, 5
Bonnifield, M.S., 56, 57
Bony Canyon, 22
boomtowns, 8
Boulder (Hoover) Dam, 98
Bradley, Lewis R. "Broadhorns," 31, 46
Bragg, Allen C., 61–62, 109, 136
Broadhead, Michael J., 49
Broken Hills (firm), 92
Bryan, William Jennings, 53, 64
Buchanan, James, 43
Buck, Franklin A., 30, 39, 43
Buckaroo Hall of Fame, 113
Buckingham, Fritz, 112
Buena Vista Canyon, 21, 22
Bullionville, 41, 44
Bureau of Indian Affairs, 71
Bureau of Land Management (BLM), 107, 129, 130, 148
Bureau of Reclamation, 110
Burning Man festival, 3
Butler, Jim, 36

Caliente, 97, 99–101, 149
Caliente Railroad Depot, *79*
California, 6, 15, 16, 18, 30, 53–54
California Trail, 16
California Trail Interpretive Center (Elko), *84*, 122
cantaloupes, 68
Carlin, 29, 123
Carson City–Reno, 6, 73
Carson River, 56
Carson Sink valley, 71
Carter, Jimmy, 103
Cassidy, George W., 52
Catholics, 139–140
cattle industry: in Elko, 30–31; in Great Basin, 59; overview

of, 6; in Pioche, 42–43; sheep industry compared to, 128–29
cattlemen, 27, 59, 113, 122, 128–29, 150
caves, 94
central corridor, 35–50, 53
Central Pacific Railroad (CPRR): challenges to, 115; completion of, 19; construction of, 25, 26–27, 29–30; economic impact of, 6; financial crisis, 33–34; along Humboldt, 59; Humboldt Trail as route for, 25; impact of, 32–34; as largest property owner, 58; university land donated by, 31
"charcoal burners" war, 143
charcoal ovens, 48, *86*
cheatgrass, 127, 128
"checkerboard lands" alongside railroads, 32–33, 58
Cherry Creek, 87, 95, 96
Chinese laborers, 26
Christian settlers, 24
Churchill Arts Council, 74
Churchill County, 20, 65–74, *151t*
Civilian Conservation Corps (CCC), 68
Civil War, 23, 54, 58, 142
Clark, W.A., 97, 99, 100
Clark County, 46, 97, 104, 108
Clark's railroad, 97, 100, 115, 125
Clemens, Orion, 18–19, 21
Clemens, Samuel L. (Mark Twain): as journalist, 23, 100, 132; as prospector, 21, 147; travels west, 18–19; Unionville visited by, 20, 22
Cleveland, A.C., 60
Cloud, Barbara, 131
coal-fired power, 95

Cobre line, 88

Cold War, 71, 102

colleges and universities, 31, 73, 120–21

Colorado River tributaries, 40

Combined Metals Reduction Co. (CMR), 98

The Coming of the Frontier Press (Cloud), 131

Commercial Hotel (Elko), 116

communities, 7, *10*

community colleges, 73, 120

company towns, 89–90

Comstock Lode: aftermath of heyday, 63; discovery of, 139; Eureka compared to, 46; mills of, 70; Pioche compared to, 42; rush to, 54

Connor, Patrick, 41

Conquered Provinces (Townley), 101–2

Consolidated Copper Company, 90

copper industry, 53, 87–88, 90–91, 111–12

counties: demographics, *151t*; establishment and boundaries of, 20; maps, *9*

courthouses. *See also under county or city name, e.g.:* Battle Mountain: courthouse: building, 20; scandals involving, 45–46; as symbols, 7; wooden, 72, 149

cowboys, 27, 59, 113, 122, 128–29, 150

crime, 22, 42

Crocker, Charles, 26, 27, 115

Crosby, Bing, 116

Crumley, Lee, 116

Crumley, Newton, 116

Crystal Springs, 37

cultural evolution (local level), 7

cultural institutions, 72–74

Culverwell, Charles, 99

Daggett, Rollin, 32

Dahl, Albin B., 117

dairy operations, 68

Deep Ruth Shaft (Ely), *80*

Delamar gold camp, 102

DeLongchamps, Frederick, 110

demographics: in early statehood, 54–55; Nevada and other states compared, 63; religious breakdown, 140; school-age population, 138; turn-of-century (1900), *64t*; twentieth century to present, *151t*

DeQuille, Dan, 23, 100, 132

Derby Dam, 66

Desert Challenge (Lillard), 6

Desert Land Act, 1877, 59, 62

Donald C. Reynolds conglomerate, 136

Donner's Party crossing, 1846, 16, 26

Donner Summit, 115

drought, 1886–1889, 60, 62, 63

drought, 1928–1932, 60

Dun Glen, 54

early warning system, 69

earthquake, 1954, 74

earthquake, 2008, *83*, 123

Earthtones (Ronald and Trimble), 3–4

economic diversification, 8, 91, 92

education, 55, 110, 136–39

Egan, Howard, 17–18, 19

Eisenhower Freeway (Interstate 80), 19, 112, 113, 146, 149–50 electricity, 88, 98

Elko: attractions, 117; Battle Mountain compared to, 28; Big Meadows compared to, 110; California Trail Interpretive Center, *84*, 122; Carlin compared to, 29; Central Pacific Railroad (CPRR) impact on, 32; Chamber of Commerce, *77*; as commercial and political hub, 30–31; courthouse, 118, 119; current conditions, 150; economic conditions in, 8; establishment of, 29; gold mining in, 114; as livestock town, 3; museums, *82*; newspapers in, 132–33; state university establishment in, 31; as urban island, 5

Elko County, 30, 115–24

Elko Free Press (newspaper), 133

Elko Independent (newspaper), 132

Elliott, Russell R., 39, 90

Ely: architecture, 150; charcoal ovens near, *86*; as commercial center, 88, 89; as county seat, 40; courthouse, 92; current conditions, 149, 150; economic conditions, 91, 92; ethnic diversity in, 92–93; mining industry in, 3, *80*; museums, *79*; newspapers in, 133–35; railroad connection to, 88

Ely, John, 41–42

Ely (Robinson) District, 87, 88–89, 90, 91

Ely–Ruth–McGill triad, 90

emigrants, travels of, 26

endangered species protection, 107

entertainment, 3, 116–17

Entsminger, John, 108

Environmental Protection Agency, 91

Episcopalians, 139, 142

Esmeralda County, 20

ethnic diversity, 92–93

Eureka: artistic images, 49; current conditions, 149; economic conditions, 46–49; gold mining in, 114; newspapers, 135; Opera House, 47, 49, *85*; passage to, 29

Eureka and Its Resources (Molinelli), 47

Eureka and Palisade Railroad (E&P), 48, 88

Eureka County, 47, 49

evangelical groups, 139

Fallon: agriculture in, 67; courthouse, 72, 149; current conditions, 149; economic conditions, 8; growth and development of, 66, 68; military operations in, 68–70; as urban island, 5

Fallon, Mike, 66

Fallon Center, 73

Fallon Paiute-Shoshone Colony, 71

Fallon Paiute-Shoshone Reservation, 71

federal government, 7–8, 129–30

Federal Land Policy Management Act (FLPMA), 129–30

Fernley, 70

"Fish Creek Massacre," 1879, 48

Fisher, Marion, 117

flash floods, 100

Fleischmann Foundation, 73, 93, 121

floods, 70

Fort Halleck, 54

Fort McDermit, 54

Fort Ruby, 54
forts, government grants to, 7
Forty-Mile Desert, 5, 16, 21, 27
fraternal orders, 143–44
Fremont, John, 16
Frenchman's Ford, 27. *See also*
Winnemucca
Freudenthal, Herman E., 135
frontier thesis, 4–5, 148–49

gambling: in Jackpot, 124; Nevada
reputation for, 3; prominence
of, 147; regulation and taxation
of, 117; in West Wendover, 123,
124
Gass, Octavius D., 37
ghost towns: description of, 50;
identification of, 124; and junk-
yards, 96; "other Nevadas" as,
8; overview of, 3; towns escap-
ing fate of, 25, 46
Ghost Train of Old Ely, 93
Ginn, John I., 57
Goin, Peter, 127
Goldfield: bonanza, fading of, 88;
gold found at, 53, 87; as Mojave
Desert town, 5; promotion of,
89; rush to, 112
Gold Hill mines, 39
gold mines and mining: bonanza,
47, 114; in California, 16, 30;
in Elko County, 117–19; increasing importance of, 113;
prospecting, 21, 41, 117; reports
and discovery, 16, 117–18; yield,
43, 48
gold prices, 119
Gordon, Laura DeForce, 56, 57
Goshute Indian Reservation, 18
Gould, George, 115
governor's race, 1902, 60
grandmothers' quilting projects, 8

Great Basin: aquifer, 107; current
conditions, 149; descriptions
of, 109; earthquakes in, 123;
grazing terrain in, 59; land distribution policy impact on, 58;
maps, *10–12*; metals industry in,
87; Mojave Desert, blending in
with, 104; Native Americans in,
54–55; passageways across, 14–
19; telegraph spanning, 18–19;
topography of, 5
Great Basin College, 120–21
Great Basin National Park, *85*, 93–
95, 96, 106
Great Basin Water Network
(GBNW), 107
Great Basin Water Network v. Taylor,
106
Great Depression, 68, 90, 91, 98,
129
"Great East," 20, 22
Great Recession: aftermath of, 8;
county populations, impact on,
108; education, impact on, 121,
139; Elko County during, 118,
119; higher education, impact
on, 73
Gridley, Reuel C., 23
"Gridley's Sack of Flour," 23–24
Growing Up in a Company Town
(Elliott), 90
Guggenheim family, 88–89
Gund, George, 122

Hall, Shawn, 124
Hamilton, 39, 40, 42, 87
Harrell, Andrew J., 60
Hickson, Howard, 121
high schools, 137
Highway 40, 19, 113, 146
Highway 50 (a.k.a. Lincoln
Highway), 14, 19, 149

Highway 93, 149
highways: along Humboldt River, 19; construction of, 146; interstate, 16, 19, 112, 113, 146, 149–50; promotion of, *80*, 112
Hiko, 38, 101–2
Homestead Act, 1862, 58
Hoover, Herbert, 99
Hoover Dam, 98
Howard, Anne, 126
Hudson's Bay Company, 14
Hughes, Howard, 120
Humboldt, Alexander von, 16
Humboldt Basin, 15, 16, 56
Humboldt corridor/region: economic conditions, 115; impressions of, 30; mining rush in, 21; Native Americans in, 53, 54; towns along, 35
Humboldt County: economic conditions, 110–11, 113; establishment of, 20; promotion of, 136; reform movements, 110; travels in, 61–62
Humboldt County Museum, Winnemucca, *84*
Humboldt River: Central Pacific Railroad (CPRR) along, 27, 59; dams on, 110; economic conditions along, 61–64; exploration of, 14; highways along, 19; recollections of, 16; tributaries of, 17, 18
Humboldt–Toiyabe National Forest, 148
Humboldt Trail, 14–17, 25, 26–34, *151t*
Humphrey, William B., 113
Huntington, Collis P., 34

immigrants, 26, 27, 47–48, 92–93, 140, 143

industrial revolution, 89
Internet, 131, 136, 147
Interstate 80 (Eisenhower Freeway), 19, 112, 113, 146, 149–50
interstate highways, 16
Ione, 35
Irish Catholics, 140
Irish Mountain mines, 37–38, 101
Irving, Washington, 15
Italian immigrants, 48, 140, 143

Jackpot, 124
James, Ronald, 92, 99
Jews, 142–43
Jones, John P., 32, 64, 111

Kennecott Copper Company, 90, 91, 96
Kimberly: former site of, 92; mining industry in, 89, 90
Korean War, 69, 89, 90, 98

labor unions, 91
Lahontan Dam, 67
Lahontan Reservoir, 70
Lake Tahoe, 70
Lambert, Darwin, 95
Lander, Frederick W., 22
Lander County: boundaries, shift in, 47; courthouse, *83*, 114; establishment of, 20; naming of, 22; population, 114; as prospect jumping-off point, 23
land policies, 51
land use maps, *13*
Las Vegas: economic slump, 118; establishment of, 46, 97; growth and development, 104, 105; Pahranagat Valley compared to, 102; region, 6, 37; towns, other emulating, 150; water use, 104, 105, 107–8

Las Vegas Valley Water District
  (LVVWD), 105, 106
Laxalt, Paul, 120
Laxalt, Robert, 3
Lee, Francis and Jane, *76*
Lehman, Absalom, 94
lesser-known cities, 4
Lewis, Oscar, 24, 25
libraries, 72–73, 119–20, 131
Life Among the Paiutes (Winnemucca), 55
Lillard, Richard, 6
Lincoln, President, 46, 130
Lincoln County: courthouse, 99;
  current conditions, 149; establishment of, 37; population,
  104–5; revival in, 97–99; seat
  of, 42–43; threat to, 105; water
  transferred from, 106
Lincoln County Conservation,
  Recreation, and Development
  Act, 106
Lincoln Highway (a.k.a. Highway
  50), 14, 19, 149
livestock industry: cattle drives,
  78; cattlemen *versus* sheepherders, 128–29; challenges,
  63, 64; cheatgrass spread
  through, 128; critique of, 126–
  27; dominant figures, 59–60,
  61, 89; economic impact of, 113;
  evolution of, 6–7; federal regulation of, 129–30; grazing, 59;
  halls of fame, 113; herd transport, 59; in Pershing County,
  110; towns, 3
livestock owners, land for, 33
local culture, 7
local government, 72–74
local history, 6
local newspapers, 135
local writers, 4

Long, Walter S., 49
long-distance telephoning, 136, 147
Los Angeles, 46, 107
Los Angeles Department of Water
  and Power (LADWP), 95
Lovelock: agriculture in, 62–63;
  Central Pacific Railroad (CPRR)
  impact on, 32; courthouse, 110;
  current conditions, 150; Fallon
  compared to, 66; population,
  109; prospects, 109–10
Lovelock, George, 27

Mackedon, Michon, 72
Magma Copper, 92
Manogue, Father Patrick, 139
Marschall, John P., 142–43
Martin, Anne, 125, 126
Masons, 143–44
Max C. Fleischmann Foundation,
  73, 93, 121
McCarran, Pat, 68, 134
McCormick, James C., 49
McGill, 90, 91, 96
McGill, William, 61, 89
McKinley, William, 64
Meadow Valley, 40
Meadow Valley Wash, 100
mechanical arts, 31
media, modern, 149
metals, precious, 41
Methodists, 139, 142
minerals, extraction of, 98
mines and mining: collapse of,
  46; establishment of, 41–42;
  future of, 147; during Great
  Depression, 98; immigrant
  labor, 47–48; inspections, 38;
  during Korean War, 89, 90;
  mining rush, 21; Mormons and,
  150; production, 22; prospects,
  22–23; revival of, 63–64, 92,

125; ruins of, 49–50; stagnation of, 87; taxation of, 31, 119; technology, 92; from World War II to Korean War, 98
missionary work, 142
Mission Revival depot, 100
Mojave Desert, 5, 104, 105
Molinelli, Lambert, 47
monetary policy, 51–53, 110
Monroe, Warren L., 132–33
Morgan, Dale, 16
Mormon Church, 107, 126
Mormons: attitudes toward, 45, 140; mining activity, attitudes concerning, 40–41, 150; in North-Center, 139; overview of, 140–41; in Pahranagat Valley, 101, 102; in Panaca, 40, 43–46, 97; Pioche, attitudes concerning, 43; as sheepherders, 129; towns, 44
"Mormon War," 1857, 41
motels, 146
motorists, Basin crossing routes available to, 14
mountain ranges, 12, 17
Mt. Moriah, 106
Muir, John, 4, 49–50
museums: in Churchill County, 73; courthouses as, 99; in Elko, 82, 122; in Ely, 79; in White Pine County, 93; in Winnemucca, 84
MX missile, 103–4

national historic landmarks, 93
National Lead Co., 98
national parks, 85, 93–95, 96, 106
National Reclamation Act, 1902, 66
Native Americans: in agriculture, 101; Anglos aided by, 17; battles, 28, 54; in Churchill County, 70–71; conquest and

displacement of, 53–55; handicrafts, 71; killing of, 15; missionary work with, 142; near Fallon, 69; policies toward, 51; political activists, 55; population, 56; reservations, 3, 18, 70, 71; subcultures of, 8; water rights, 70
natural resources, protecting, 130
nature, beauty of, 50
Naval Air Station Fallon, 68–70, 73
Nellis Air Force Base, 104
Nevada, popular image of, 3
Nevada boundary shift, 36–37
Nevada Central Railroad, 29
Nevada Consolidated Copper Company, 88, 89, 90
Nevada Constitution, 119, 125–26, 130
Nevada Department of Museums and History, 93
Nevada Division of Environmental Protection (NDEP), 105
Nevada Historical Society, 131
Nevada Northern depot, 93
Nevada Northern railroad, 88, 89, 93
Nevadans, history of, 5–6
Nevada population/demographics. See demographics
Nevada statehood, 36, 46
Nevada State Museum, 121
Nevada Supreme Court, 106
Nevada Territory, 20–25
Nevada Test Site (NTS), 71, 102, 104
New Deal, 7–8, 68
Newlands, Francis G., 65–66
Newlands Project: courthouses built after authorization of, 72; economic impact of, 125; museum exhibits on, 73; overview of, 8, 65–68; water supply for,

71; weather and river flow impact on, 70

Newmont Mining Co., 118

newspapers, 131–36

Nixon, George, 52, 53, 111, 112, 136

the North-Center: agriculture in, 127; description and overview of, 4–6; federal government impact on, 7–8; history of, 6–8; impressions of, 118; land policies affecting, 58, 130; livestock industry in, 61, 127; Native Americans in, 56; population, 63, 64t; schools in, 138; silver crusade activists in, 52; woman suffrage movement in, 56

North Central Nevada Historical Society, 61

Northeastern Nevada Historical Society, 121

Northeastern Nevada Museum (Elko), 82, 121–22

northern European immigrants, 27

Northern Nevada Railway, 88, 89, 93

Northern Nevada Railway Museum, 79

Northern Paiutes, 15, 53

Nothing Like It in the World (Ambrose), 26

nuclear testing, 71–72, 102

Nye, James W., 19, 35, 54

Nye County, 35, 36, 105, 106

Oats Park Art Center, 73–74, 77

Odd Fellows, 143–44

Oddie, Tasker L., 29, 145–46

Oddie–Colton Public Domain Highway Act, 146

Off-Highway Vehicle (OHV) gathering, 114

Ogden, Peter Skene, 14, 17, 94

"Ogden's River" (name), 15, 16

Old Heart of Nevada (Hall), 124

Orr Ditch settlement, 1944, 70

Osceola, 87

"the other Nevada" (term), 3, 4, 8, 150

Overland Mail, 20

Overland Stage, 19

Overland Stage line, 65

Owens Valley water, transfer of, 107

Pacific Railway Act, 58

Pahranagat district, 41

Pahranagat Mountains, 100

Pahranagat Valley, 37–38, 101–2

Paiutes, 15, 53, 54, 55, 101

Panaca: Caliente compared to, 99; current conditions, 149; description of, 40, 43–44; economic conditions, 44–45; establishment of, 43–44; Pioche, relations with, 45, 97, 98–99; settlers, 76

Paradise Valley, 27–28

parks, 85, 93–95, 96, 106, 112

Peabody, Elizabeth, 55

Peabody Report, 138

Pershing County, 61, 110

Pioche: Caliente compared to, 99; courthouse, 45–46; current conditions, 149; description of, 40; economic conditions in, 41–43, 97; inhabitants of, 41, 44; mining industry in, 42, 97, 98; newspapers, 135–36; Panaca, relations with, 45, 97, 98–99; railroad connection to, 100

Pioche, Francois L.A., 42

Pioneer Hotel (Elko), 78

Pittman, Key, 133, 134

Pittman, Vail, 133–34
poetry, 122
polygamy, 45, 140
Pony Express: cabins, 121; churches in, 24; historic overview of, 18–19; resting places, 20; riders, prospecting by, 22; trails explored by, 14, 25
Populist Party, 53
postal roads, 145
potatoes, 112
poultry operations, 68
prehistoric people, 5, 73
presidential election, 1900, 64
prisons, 95–96, 145
Project Shoal, 71–72
Protestants, 141–42
public education, 137, 138–39
public lands, 7, 130
public schools, 33
Pyramid Lake Indian Reservation, 70
Pyramid Lake War, 54

Quadra Mining Ltd., 92
quilting projects, 8

railroads: construction, 26–27, 32–33, 46, 97; depots, 79; economic impact of, 113, 115–16; efficiency of, 112; freight-hauling rates, 32; government grants to, 7; maps, 11; museums, 79; restoration, 93; stations, 26–34; through Humboldt Basin, 16
Rainbow Canyon, 100
ranches, 3
Rathbun, Daniel C.B., 54
Raymond, William, 41–42
Raymond & Ely (R & E) Mine, 41–42

Reagan, Ronald, 94, 103
recession, 2008–2010. See Great Recession
recession, early 1920s, 90, 126–27
Reese River, 18
Reese River district, 23
Reese River Reveille (newspaper), 23, 24
Reese River Valley, 24–25
reform movements, 57
Reid, Harry, 95, 106
religious organizations, 139–43
Reno, 26, 27, 31, 70, 150
Requa, Mark, 88, 89
Rickard, Tex, 89
Ring, Orvis, 137
river diversion projects, 27
rivers, maps of, 12
roads, 145–46
Roaring Twenties, 90
Robbins, John E., 117
Robinson District, 87, 88–89, 90, 91
Rocky Mountain Fur Company, 17
Ronald, Ann, 3–4
Roosevelt, Franklin D., 129
Roosevelt, Theodore, 66
Roughing It (Twain), 21
Ruby Mountains, 58–59
Ruby Valley Treaty, 54
rural Nevada memories, 4
Russell, Charles, 134, 138
Ruth, 88, 89, 90, 91, 92
Rye Patch Dam, 110

Sacramento Pass, 17
The Sagebrush Ocean (Trimble), 5
Sagebrush Rebellion, 8, 130
Salt Lake City, 6, 43, 46
Sand Springs, 72
Sanitary Fund, 23–24

San Pedro, Los Angeles and Salt Lake Railroad (SP, LA & SL RR), 97, 100, 115, 125
Scanlon, Lawrence, 140
schools, 33, 136–39
Scrugham, James G., 94
secret orders, 143
sheepherders: cattlemen compared to, 128–29; descendants of, 120; job opportunities for, 59; in Paradise Valley, 28; role, reduced for, 150; sheep transport for, 65
sheep industry, 6, 30–31, 42–43, 59, 128–29
Sherman Station, 77
Shoshone, 53, 54
Sierra Club, 49
silver coinage suspension, 1873, 51, 52
silver crusade, 51–53, 110
Silver League, 52–53
silver mines and mining, 30, 40, 47, 48
Silver Party, 111
silver price, drop in, 42, 51
Simpson, James H., 18, 19
Simpson Park Mountains, 18
smaller towns, 4
Smith, Jedediah, 17
Snake Range, 58–59, 82, 94
Snake Valley, 95
Snow, Erastus, 41
Snyder, E.H. (Ed), 98
southeastern Nevada, rural, 103–4
Southern Baptists, 142
Southern Nevada Water Authority (SNWA), 106
Southern Pacific (SPRR): Central Pacific Railroad (CPRR) taken over by, 34; challenges and competition, 115, 116; connections to, 88; as railroad spur to, 66; route of, 128
Southern Paiutes, 101
SP, LA & SL RR (Clark's railroad), 97, 100, 115, 125
Sparks, 70
Sparks, John, 59–60
Spring Creek, 123
Spring Valley, 106
Starrs, Paul F., 127
state government, attitudes toward, 7
state prison, 95–96, 145
state university, 31
Steep Trails (Muir), 49
Steninger, E.M., 133
Stewart, Helen, 97, 102
Stewart, William M., 32, 64, 111
Stillwater, 65, 70–71
Stitser, Rollin C., 136
Stokes, Anson Phelps, 29
Stokes Castle, 24, 86
Storey County, 30, 63
subcultures, 3, 89–92, 150
sugar beets, 67

Taylor, 87
Taylor Grazing Act, 1934, 129
teacher training, 137
Tea Party movement, 52
telegraph, 18–19, 132
telephone service, 136, 146–47
television, 136
Te-moak (Shoshone chief), 54
Territorial Enterprise (newspaper), 23, 132
Thousand Springs, 59
Tinnan, John, 59–60
Tonopah: bonanza, fading of, 88; as county seat, 35, 36;

discoveries at, 53, 87; discovery of, 36; as Mojave Desert town, 5
TOPGUN (NAS Fallon), 69
tourism, 104, 116–17, 147
Townley, John, 62–63, 101–2, 109
towns: along Humboldt Trail, 27; company, 89–90; Las Vegas emulated by, 150; maps, 10; Mormon towns, 44; small, 4
The Town That Died Laughing (Lewis), 24
"traveling stones" tale, 101
Treasure City, 39, 87
Trimble, Stephen, 3–4, 5
Truckee–Carson Irrigation District (TCID), 68, 70
Truckee Meadows, 28, 109
Truckee River, 26, 54, 66, 67, 70
Turner, Frederick Jackson, 4, 148–49
Tuscarora, 123
Twain, Mark (Samuel L. Clemens): as journalist, 23, 100, 132; as prospector, 21, 147; travels west, 18–19; Unionville visited by, 20, 22

underground nuclear testing, 72
Union Pacific, 26, 29–30, 100, 123
Unionville, 20–22, 28
universities, 31
University of Nevada, Reno, 120
University Preparatory School (Elko), 120
U.S. Fish and Wildlife Service, 71
U.S. Forest Service, 130, 148
U.S. Highway 40, 19, 113, 146
U.S. Highway 93, 149
U.S. Reclamation Service (USRS), 66–67, 68

U.S. Route 50 (a.k.a. Lincoln Highway), 14, 19, 149
U.S. Supreme Court, 70
U.S. v. Orr Ditch, 67
Utah War, 43, 140

Veteran, 89, 90
Vietnam conflict, 69
Virginia City, 39
vocational and industrial training, 137–38

Wadsworth, 26
Walker, Joseph R., 15, 53–54
Wallace, Charles C. "Black," 52
Wanamaker, H. V. (Jack), 121
Ward, 87
Warren, Earl, 121
Washburn Ranch Cattle Drive, 78
Washoe County, 63
water conservation and recycling, 108
water management, 65–66
water policies, 51, 70, 71
water war, 1920–2015, 104–8
Wells, 29, 32, 83, 123
Western Folklife Center (Elko), 78, 122
Western Nevada Community College (WNCC), 73
Western Pacific Railroad (WPRR), 115–16
West Wendover, 123–24
wetlands, 71
Wheat, Margaret, 71
Wheeler Peak, 17, 85, 94
White Pine County: copper found in, 53; establishment of, 40; historic and nature preservation in, 92–95; mining industry in, 87–92; population, 91, 104;

threat to, 105; water war, participation in, 106
White Pine County Public Museum, 93
White Pine district, 38
White Pine Historical Foundation, 93
White Pine Land and Livestock Company, 141
White Pine Mountains, 30, 36, 38–40
White Pine region, 37, 52
Wiegand Foundation of Nevada, 122
wildlife refuges, 70, 71
Wingfield, George, 53, 111–12, 129
Wingfield Park, 112
Winnemucca: Big Meadows compared to, 110; Central Pacific Railroad (CPRR) impact on, 32; current conditions, 150; economic conditions in, 8; livestock industry in, 3, 78; museums, 84; name origin, 27; newspapers, 136; opera house, 112; population, 28, 109; prospects, 110–13; railroad station at, 27–28; as urban island, 5
Winnemucca (Paiute chief), 27
Winnemucca, Sarah, 55, 75, 110
"Winnemucca to the Sea" highway, promotion of, 80, 112
woman suffrage, 51, 56–57, 110, 125–27
Woodruff Manifesto, 140
World War I, 67, 90
World War II: air bases, 123; copper industry during, 90; in Fallon, 68–69; innovations following, 146; mining industry during, 98; railroad industry during, 100
Wren, Thomas, 52

A Yankee Trader in the Goldrush (Buck), 30
Yerington, 3
Young, Brigham, 17–18

Zanjani, Sally, 55
Zion's Cooperative Mercantile Institution (ZCMI), 44